Andrew A.

THE GOOD PASTOR

Andrew A. Bonar

THE GOOD PASTOR

Edited by his daughter

MARJORY BONAR

AMBASSADOR

BELFAST ◆ **GREENVILLE**
NORTHERN IRELAND ◆ SOUTH CAROLINA

Andrew Bonar - The Good Pastor
This edition 1999

ISBN 1 84030 045 0

Ambassador Publications
a division of
Ambassador Productions Ltd.
Providence House
16 Hillview Avenue,
Belfast, BT5 6JR
Northern Ireland

Emerald House
1 Chick Springs Road, Suite 203
Greenville,
South Carolina 29609, USA
www.emeraldhouse.com

CONTENTS

CONTENTS

INTRODUCTION

THE reminiscences of our father, and the letters contained in this volume have been gathered from many sources, with the kind help of friends to whom I desire to express my gratitude. The sermons and addresses are taken in part from his own manuscript, and in part from the notes of hearers. The only two addresses which have had the benefit of his own revision are those on *Angel Workers* and on *What gives Assurance*, both of which were published some years ago in tract form. As the Diary was the disclosure of our father's inner life, these reminiscences will, it is hoped, recall, however imperfectly, that outer life which was known and read by the world through which he walked in the narrow path that leads to life.

'He being dead yet speaketh.' His memory is still an incentive to holiness. While he lived others said of him, 'I never met him without being the better for it.' The secret lay in his everyday fellowship with the Lord. He looked not at the things which are seen, but at the things which are not seen.

Born in Edinburgh in 1810, he was carefully and lovingly trained by godly parents in all the things that concern salvation, but he speaks of himself as being still without Christ till he was twenty years of age. When reading such books as Doddridge's *Rise and Progress of Religion in the Soul*, he used to feel seriously impressed ; and the preaching of Edward Irving ' cast into his soul some of the first beams of light as to spiritual truth.' But what more than anything else impressed him, was to see one and another of his friends coming to Christ ; then he longed to know that he too was born again. The great change seems to have come to him more gradually than suddenly, not in a time of revival, but in the solitude of his own room. On Sabbath, the 17th of October, 1830, while quietly sitting in a room for study which he shared with his brothers, reading Guthrie's *Trial of a Saving Interest in Christ*, he began to have a ' secret joyful hope,' that he really believed on the Lord Jesus. The fulness and freeness of divine grace filled his heart. ' *I did nothing but receive,*' he says. No doubt of his acceptance in Christ ever again dimmed the clearness of his faith. Thirty years afterwards he wrote : ' I have been many many times unhappy for a time, but never led to doubt my interest in the Lord Jesus.' Again he says : ' For fifty years the Lord has kept me within sight of the Cross,' and his testimony after sixty years of life in Christ is, that the Lord has never once left him in darkness as to his interest in Him, all these years. Along with this clear sense of forgiveness he seems to have obtained a vivid apprehension of his union to Christ. His faith rested, not so much on the truth about the Lord Jesus Christ, as on His Person ; and in His living companionship he walked all the days of his life. He once related an incident of his student days, which must have made a great impression upon him, as he told it with much feeling. In his daily walk to one of the college classes he and his companions used to meet an old man going to business, who was sometimes walking along holding his hat a little way off his head. The peculiarity of the action excited the notice of those who met him, and some one asked the old man what he meant by it. He was at first reluctant to tell, but at last he said, 'Well, if you will know, I will tell you. As I walk along the street I have sometimes such fellowship with the Lord Jesus, that I feel as if He were close beside me, and I lift my hat in token of reverence.' Of his own experience our father wrote on his eighty-second birthday: 'It was in the year 1830 that I found the Saviour, or rather, that He found me and laid me on His shoulders rejoicing, and I have never parted company with Him all these sixty-two years.' While others were stumbling at dark doctrines, or searching into the depths of their heart's sinfulness, or looking within for signs of their regeneration, he was pressing on in a life of rejoicing and ever nearer fellowship with Him whose voice at the first had whispered in His ear, 'Son, be of good cheer, thy sins are forgiven thee.' He was inclined naturally to depression. Humiliation and self-abasement were everyday exercises of his spiritual life. The more striking was the current of joy that flowed steadily and without change all through his life. Sorrow fell to his lot. Disappointment chilled his hopes. Deeper waters crossed his pathway than even those nearest him ever knew. They only heard the song with which he praised Him who had delivered him from all evil.

It is interesting to notice in connection with his conversion that William Guthrie, who wrote the *Trial of a Saving Interest in Christ,* owed the deepening, if not the beginning, of his spiritual life to Samuel Rutherford, under whom he studied in St. Andrews. If our father's religious life was modelled on that of another, it was on the life of the Reformers and Covenanters. He studied their writings and drank in much of their spirit. He had something of their strength and reality of purpose, the same fidelity to truth,—though with perhaps more love and less fiery vehemence,—often the same quaint habit of speech, and the same fervour of spirit which would have led him to lay down his life for the Lord he loved. Like John Welsh he spent hours in wrestling prayer for those who cared not to plead for themselves. Like Samuel Rutherford his one desire was to get a deeper insight into the love of the 'only lovely' Lord Jesus. The words of a Reformer and martyr, 'We have a good and gentle Lord, let us follow His steps,' might have been his own. He did not find it hard to unite a reverent belief in the most solemn and mysterious truths of the Bible with a joyous and triumphant hope. One who knew him well has written of him: 'Calvinism and the evangelical creed were never so fairly (their critics might say insidiously) recommended, as by this man who stood by every doctrine, even the most severe and difficult to believe, while he seemed to live in a perpetual sunshine, and to spread not gloom, but brightness and good-nature wherever he appeared.' ' I believe everything that is in the Confession of Faith,' are his own words, ' but I believe more than is in it ; for Jordan may overflow his banks.' Some might smile at his unquestioning faith, but there was none who did not envy him his unfailing gladness and unbroken serenity.

His conscientiousness led him, while still a student, to postpone his entrance on his studies in the Divinity Hall. ' I always kept back till I was in Christ before I could think of entering the Hall.' In 1831—a year after his conversion—he passed through the preparatory examination before the Presbytery, and his theological studies began. Left fatherless when only eleven years of age, he, along with his brothers and sisters, clung closely to the mother who was so worthy of their love and reverence, and looked up to their oldest brother James as the representative of the father who had been taken from them. Our father's name can hardly be dissociated from the names of his two older brothers, John and Horatius. Both of them were in the ministry before him, Horatius only a year earlier, and John some years before. Through a long life of service, they followed the same course, preaching the same truths, bearing the same testimony, each with his own special characteristics. His brother John, though less widely known than his two brothers, was distinguished for his culture and scholarship, and for the eloquence and grace of his preaching. He had an immense fund of humour, and held quite a unique place among his friends, with his genial kindliness and exuberant flow of spirits. His loving interest in the spiritual welfare of his younger brother is brought out in our father's Diary and in much of their early correspondence with each other.

A band of devoted men were at that time preparing for the ministry, of whom some remain unto this present day, but the most are fallen asleep. One of the survivors of that circle of friends, Dr. Moody-Stuart, writes of their early intercourse :—

'My introduction to your father was in 1836, through his attached friend Robert M'Cheyne, when they were still students for the ministry. Robert M'Cheyne's father and family were members of the congregation to which I ministered before I was ordained, when St. Luke's was about to be built. It was to me a golden day when I first became acquainted with a young man so full of Christ. He introduced Andrew Bonar and then Horace and Somerville, and I invited them to meet in my house once a week for prayer. It was a singularly pleasant and fruitful meeting, for we were of one heart and one mind, and the Lord Jesus, according to His promise, was in the midst of us with the joy of His salvation.

'Five years later, when Andrew was minister at Collace and M'Cheyne at Dundee, they sometimes met at Annat for conference and prayer. There is still fresh in my memory one bright forenoon, when we sat together in the garden-seat in heavenly fellowship, and not without the joy of the Holy Ghost. This early communion with them both I hope soon to renew in the heavenly inheritance, where they are now walking with the Lamb by the fountains of living waters, and with your father to remember all the way by which the Lord has led us these twice forty years in the wilderness.' Dr. Moody-Stuart's recollections of our father are of 'his unfailing buoyancy of brightness through his daily rejoicing in the Lord. The joy of the Lord was his strength, with a fulness and a constancy that were quite singular.'

In 1838 each of that band of friends had found a sphere of labour. Our father's settlement at Collace followed a short assistantship at Jedburgh and some months of missionary work in the parish of St. George's Church, Edinburgh. The times were peculiar, and God raised up men of peculiar grace, mighty in the Scriptures, full of the Holy Ghost and of faith. Darkness covered the land spiritually. The Gospel, because little preached, was little sought for. Like the sun bursting through the clouds came the great revival of 1839-40, which spread all over the land. Then followed, in 1843, the memorable Disruption, when, for conscience' sake, more than four hundred ministers of Christ severed their connection with the Established Church and formed the Free Church of Scotland. The effects of this event upon our father's work in Collace were in all respects for the better. He was left free to work as he chose among his people, and even during the trying time when they were without a church in which to worship, God's presence was felt among them, quickening and blessing. His marriage in 1848 increased his usefulness as a pastor, and brought to him new and deeper experiences of life. His later years at Collace seem to have cost him many anxious thoughts and much searching of heart. The full tide of revival had ebbed, and the work of God was not so apparent as in earlier years. His sorrowful reflections in his Diary on this account recall a story he often used to tell in connection with a good old minister at the close of last century. Being much discouraged by the small attendance at the prayer-meeting, the old man one day added to the intimation of the time and place of meeting the sorrowful remark, 'But I need hardly tell you, for none of you will be there.' As the people dispersed, they said to each other, 'The minister is vexed, we'll go this time;' and when the good man drew near the place of meeting, he saw with amazement that many were gathering together. 'How often,' he said to himself, 'have I come here with a sermon and found no congregation, and now I have come without a sermon and find a great congregation!' Retiring for a little while to an adjoining wood, he implored the Lord to give him a message and to add His blessing. Such was the power accompanying the word preached on that evening that a revival of religion began in that solemn hour, which had a mighty influence for two generations.

The people's estimate of our father's labours in Collace was very different from his own. 'When you came among us in 1839,' are their words on the occasion of his jubilee in 1888, 'Collace, as regards spiritual life, was comparatively a desert. When you left, it was like a watered garden—"a field that the Lord had blessed." The effects of your faithful testimony remain to this day, both in living souls and in the social and religious habits of the people.' His faithful preaching was continually accompanied with blessing, both in his own parish and in the many places he was in the habit of visiting. A sermon of his on 'The Pearl of Great Price' was used in a singular way. A young woman whose heart was yearning for her father's conversion had been greatly struck with this sermon, which she had heard our father preach somewhere. When he came one day to her own village, she went to the door of the vestry to ask him to preach it again, but her courage failed, and she went back into church without having asked him, but praying that he might be led to it. Her prayer was heard; the sermon she so longed for was delivered, and was the means of her father's conversion.

Eighteen years of country pastorate were years of prayer and preparation for greater work. The attraction of a call to another field of labour in Glasgow in 1856 was the attraction of harder and more extended work,—to spend the best years of life in gathering out from one dark corner of the great city a people for the Lord. Bravely he toiled on, and there, as in Collace, gales of revival came to gladden and refresh. The greatest sorrow of his life fell upon him in 1864, in the height of his usefulness, when his wife was taken from him, and he was left with his five children to journey on without her loving help and counsel. Bitter as was the sorrow, it never turned him aside from his Master's work. 'I find preaching the Word one of my best consolations,' he says at one time; and again, 'God's Lethe is in some degree fruitfulness in time of affliction.' With less to bind him to earth, he sought with more earnestness the things which are above. The loss of earthly joy brought to him more of the Saviour's presence. All his experiences combined to make him skilful in ministering to the spiritual needs of others. Especially was this felt in times of awakening. In 1839 and the years that followed he was constantly in contact with revival scenes. Very few still live to remember him as he was then, but in later times his influence was felt in every such movement. The Rev. Dr. Cuyler, of New York, writing to him in 1879, says, ' I asked our friend Moody who rendered him the most assistance in Great Britain. He answered, "The Lord Chancellor and Dr. A. A. Bonar,—the first one by attending my London meetings and giving me his powerful influence, and Dr. A. A. Bonar by helping me to deeper knowledge of the Word, and by his letters and counsels." There, my dear modest brother, is not that a jewel at least in advance from your heavenly crown?' His entire disinterestedness in this work and his single-minded desire for the glory of God and the salvation of souls were remarkable. After the revival of 1874, it was found that his congregation had received a larger share of blessing than any other in the city. But the pastor was not contented with only receiving. He rejoiced when many of his most devoted members became helpers in those different evangelistic agencies throughout the city which were the outcome of this movement, and he found it true in his own experience as well as in that of his people, that he that watereth others is watered also himself. Fresh life flowed by this means into his congregation, widening its interests and expanding its energies and sympathies. Christians from other lands were attracted to his church as they passed through Glasgow, and many a casual visitor stayed at the close of a service to express his thanks for the spiritual quickening he had received. Still more memorable were the communion seasons, when many of God's people, widely separated in their church connection, met together round the table of the Lord in Finnieston, and enjoyed a foretaste of the fellowship above which is yet to come.

Though our father's estimate of his work and of his attainments was humble, others recognised his gifts and gave him honour. The University of Edinbugh conferred on him, in 1874, the degree of Doctor of Divinity. In 1878 he, with some reluctance, allowed himself to be elected to the Moderatorship of the Assembly of the Free Church, which was held that year in Glasgow. In nominating him to the office, the retiring Moderator, Dr. Goold, made a happy allusion to the similarity of the circumstances to those of the first Assembly which met in Glasgow in 1638, at which Alexander Henderson was unanimously nominated as Moderator by the votes of his brethren—'*none being contrair except his own.*' The people of Finnieston were not behind others in doing honour to their minister. In 1881 they had celebrated his semi-jubilee as their pastor, and in 1888 a remarkable gathering was held to celebrate his fifty years' work as a minister of Christ. Representatives of the Church of God from all parts of Scotland, from England, from America, gave their testimony to the blessed influence of his words and of his writings, and to the seals God had put upon his faithful ministry.

Seven years previously, in 1881, he accepted an urgent invitation from Mr. Moody to visit America and be present at the Northfield Conference, held in the month of August. Notwithstanding his seventy-one years, he faced the discomforts of a sea voyage and the heat of an American summer, and, accompanied by his eldest daughter, spent two months on the other side of the Atlantic. He astonished his friends at Northfield by his wonderful vigour—sometimes walking two or three miles a day in the excessive heat, besides giving addresses and talking to the students and others, who listened eagerly for the weighty words that fell from his lips. Often he expressed his thankfulness to God for this visit to Northfield, and for the opportunity then given to him of enjoying fellowship with so many of God's people whose names he had long loved and honoured. He returned home with his heart glowing, and leaving behind him a fragrant memory.

The last years of his life were full of unremitting labour. He was obliged to withdraw gradually from some of his former work, but he laboured more fervently in prayers for his family, for his friends, for his congregation, for all the world. He felt himself drawing very near the world to come. 'I have been thinking to-night,' is one of the solemn entries in his Diary, 'that perhaps my next great undertaking may be this : appearing at the judgment-seat of Christ, when I give an account of my trading with my talents.' His poet-brother, Horatius, after two years of weakness and suffering, was taken home in 1889. Two years later his brother John quietly 'fell asleep,' in the eighty-ninth year of his age. And so the life-long fellowship of the three brothers was broken up ; but 'only for a season.' Our father had agreed, after much persuasion, to the appointment of a colleague, and in September 1891—the anniversary of his own ordination at Collace fifty-two years before—the Rev. D. M. M'Intyre, of College Park, London, was inducted as co-pastor and helper in his work at Finnieston. With the burden of his labours thus lightened, his friends rejoiced in the thought that years of service might yet be granted to him ; but the long, laborious life was drawing to a close. On the 30th of December 1892, he gently passed within the veil. 'He walked with God, and was not, for God took him.'

His memory is cherished by those who knew him and loved him, but by many who never saw his face he will be held in grateful remembrance for what he has written. His books are valued not for their literary merit— though he had learning and scholarship of no ordinary kind—but for the light they cast upon the Word of God and its teaching. By those who love to search the Scriptures devoutly and reverently they will always be treasured. Of his *Commentary on Leviticus*, Mr. Spurgeon writes, 'I often consult your " Leviticus," and never in vain ;' and of his other book, *Christ and his Church in the Book of Psalms*, 'Your valuable volume on the Psalms has long been in my library, and had a high place in my esteem. I have been, for some years, compiling extracts from all authors illustrating the Psalms, which extracts will be issued with my own commentary ; and I am under great obligation to you for choice pieces which I have taken the liberty to cull.'

The most widely known of his works, the *Memoir of the Rev. R. M. M'Cheyne*, is written in a simplicity of style that at once strikes the reader. Its immense circulation has made its author's name known all over the world, and many an honoured servant of Christ owes his first inspiration to the work of God to this record of a brief but blessed life. A singular blessing follows its course. A lady reading it in her house in the Highlands of Scotland finds life to her soul as she reads. An unconverted curate in the Church of England has M'Cheyne's *Sermons* sent to him by his brother. He begins to read them to his congregation, as he has been doing with others, and is amazed, after a few Sabbaths have passed, to find his people coming to him with questions about things they had never spoken of before. An American gentleman, brought to Christ while reading the *Memoir*, comes to Dundee to spend his first Sabbath in Scotland in St. Peter's, that he may worship in the church where Robert M'Cheyne used to preach. In 1845 our father's impression of the past year's work at Collace, was that little blessing had attended his ministry. 'The *Memoir of M'Cheyne* and my tract on *Baptism* seem to me the chief way in which the Lord has been using me to any extent.' How little could he then foresee the influence to be exerted in time to come by these memorials of his friend's life and ministry.

In the *Memoir* he describes Mr. M'Cheyne's preaching

as 'being in a manner the development of his soul's experience,'—'a giving out of the inward life.' The same might be said of his own. It never was his ambition to be a great preacher. He spoke to the heart of his hearers, simply and directly, not thinking of how to please them, but delivering a message from the Lord. As early as 1835 he writes : ' I never before felt the extreme difficulty of being absorbed in the desire of saving souls as my sole object, and of taking the glory of God as my simple aim. I think it is a rule of Scripture (Jeremiah i.) that, going with God's message and in His strength, we are sure to be sustained.' ' I find that simply to receive Him and wait upon Him is as difficult a matter as to speak of Him aright.' After thirty-six years of preaching ' Christ and Him crucified ' his experience is that ' Christ is more than ever precious to me in His atonement, righteousness, merit, heart. Nothing else satisfies me. I only yearn to know Him better, and preach Him more fully.' He never went to the pulpit without preparation, yet none more entirely depended on the power of the Holy Spirit to make the word preached effectual. Some of his own words in reference to Mr. M'Cheyne might with truth be applied to himself. ' There has been one among us who dwelt at the mercy-seat as if it were his home—preached the certainties of eternal life with an undoubting mind—and spent his nights and days in ceaseless breathings after holiness and the salvation of sinners. Hundreds of souls were his reward from the Lord ere he left us ; and in him have we been taught how much one man may do who will only press farther into the presence of his God, and handle more skilfully the unsearchable riches of Christ, and speak more boldly for his God.' To one was granted only a short time in which to labour, to the other a long ministry of more than fifty years; but both have heard the words, 'Well done, good and faithful servant!'

The succeeding chapters of this book have been written to bring out in detail some parts of our father's life and character, to show, not a perfect man, but one who more than most around him bore on his forehead the impress of holiness. As they read, his old hearers and those who remember his life as portrayed in these pages will recall the words of the beloved Apostle; 'And now, little children, abide in Him; that, when He shall appear, we may have confidence, and not be ashamed before Him at His coming.'

GLASGOW, 1895.

A MINISTER OF CHRIST

'Oh the peace, the quiet love, which a good man sheddeth around him! He seeketh not the haunts of crowds. He hath no one place, one time, one way of doing good; but wherever he is he findeth it, in preventing the evil; wherever there is evil, there is his vocation. He is always in his workshop, and his tools are ever at his hand; for truth and righteousness and pity and love are the tools with which he everywhere worketh the work of goodness. I start from the image which I conceive, because it doth so rebuke us all with its unseen labour and unheard-of diligence.'
—*Edward Irving.*

CHAPTER I

THE events of a ministry are not easily recalled after the lapse of sixty years. Two generations have passed away since the days when Andrew Bonar went in and out among the people of Jedburgh, but his name lingers in and around the old town, for 'the memory of the just is blessed.' There are still some who remember that their father or their mother belonged to 'Mr. Bonar's class.' It was in Jedburgh, in 1835, that he preached his first sermon, after passing through the regular course of study in the Divinity Hall of Edinburgh. There his first ministerial experiences were gained. The visitation of the prisoners in the jail gave him an insight into the evil of the human heart which he never forgot;[1] and his intercourse with Mr. Purves, his senior minister and friend, seems to have been the means of stimulating him in the study of prophetic truth, as well as in other ways. He never forgot those to whom he had ministered in Jedburgh. When staying at Hawick in 1878, he spent a day along with the Rev. Duncan Stewart in revisiting his old field of labour. Some who professed to have come to Christ during his ministry there were dear to him, and he spent a great part of the afternoon in climbing stairs and finding them out. 'He remembered every one

---

[1] 'An absent God and a present Devil' was one prisoner's account of her experience in the jail.

well, their name, their spiritual history, etc. Some had not shone for Christ so brightly as they might have done, but he did not pass them by. He had a word for each as he thought they needed. He seemed to have far greater delight in looking after these sheep that afternoon than in viewing the pleasant scenery round Jedburgh.'

One of his reminiscences of the people was a story of a half-witted man whom he used to visit. This poor man had found Christ and had learned to rejoice in the thought of His return to earth. He went to Edinburgh on a visit, and came home much dissatisfied with the ministers. When asked why, he said, 'Oh, they a' flee wi' ae wing!' They preached Christ's First, but not His Second Coming.

During his work as missionary in St. George's, Edinburgh, to which he removed at the close of 1836, Mr. Bonar's interest in the Jews was quickened by contact with several of them both in public and private. Hardly had he begun to feel at home in his first charge at Collace when he was appointed one of the four who formed a deputation in the year 1839 from the General Assembly of the Church of Scotland to the Land of Israel. This event gave a colour to all his future ministry. A stone from Mount Sinai, an olive-leaf from Gethsemane, a shell from the shores of the Lake of Galilee, a piece of Desert shittim-wood, were texts by which he made the scenes and incidents of the Bible real and living, and from which he preached the love and faithfulness of 'that same Jesus' whose feet would one day stand again upon Mount Olivet.

A beautiful incident, which he often related, occurred at Kelso when Mr. Bonar was on a visit to his brother Horatius. He was addressing a meeting there, and, when showing some ears of barley which he had plucked on Mount Zion, he said, 'If God keeps His threatenings so faithfully (Micah iii. 12), will He not keep His promises?' Next day, an old woman sent for him, and, as soon as he entered her house, she held up her hands and exclaimed, 'Oh, those ears of barley! those ears of barley!' He asked her what she meant, and she said she had just thought when he was speaking the night before that if God kept His word about ears of barley, would He not keep it about the salvation of a soul? And all her doubts fled.

The parish of Collace in Perthshire, where Mr. Bonar was ordained in 1838, lies at the foot of the hill of Dunsinnane, where once stood Macbeth's Castle, and from which there is a wide view over several counties of Scotland. The associations of the place were all in harmony with the young minister's love for everything of antiquarian interest. On the hill of Bandirran, close by Dunsinnane, are remains of a Druidic circle. A farm in the neighbourhood bears the name of Balmalcolm, and not far off is the hamlet of Cairnbeddie—'the cairn of Macbeth.' Tradition says that a green mound on the farm of Lawton is the spot where Macbeth used to administer justice. Over the doorway of the Dunsinnane burying-place in Collace churchyard is a small Saxon arch, said to have been taken from the little village of Thorngreen,[1] where once stood a house adorned by the stones of Macbeth's Castle.[2] The first Protestant minister of Collace was the Rev. James Anderson, who was ordained to the ministry of that parish in the sixteenth century. He wrote a poem entitled 'The Winter Night,'—a warning to his flock against Popery,—and dedicated it to John Erskine of

---

[1] Thorngreen, Sachar, and Kinrossie, were little villages in the parish of Collace.

[2] These details are extracted from a note-book in which Dr. Bonar has collected everything of interest connected with Collace.

Dun. When Mr. Bonar came to the parish, the old minister to whom he acted as colleague had already been there for nearly fifty years, but there was only one woman who was known to have received any good from his ministry. He was very much afraid of some one coming who would preach the 'new doctrines.' Mr. Bonar was presented to the parish through the influence of Mr. Nairne of Dunsinnane, who continued always a true friend to him and to the cause of the Free Church in the neighbourhood. Mr. Nairne, it is said, asked Mr. M'Cheyne if he would leave Dundee and come to Collace. He said 'No; but I will tell you of a much better man,' and named his friend Andrew Bonar. On hearing of his presentation to the parish, Mr. M'Cheyne wrote to him :—

'Dundee, 17th July 1838.

'MY DEAR ANDREW,—I have several times been on the very point of writing you to wish you joy of your presentation to the church of Collace. May it indeed be a gift from His hand who hath done and will do all things well. There are many tokens for good about it, so that you must feel yourself very much called by God. "Before I formed thee in the belly I knew thee ; and before thou camest forth out of the womb I sanctified thee, a prophet unto the nations." "Paul an apostle, not of man, neither by man." "*Certainly* I will be with thee, and this shall be a token unto thee that I have sent thee." All these are sweet words, for just as there is no greater misery than to run unsent, of our own private motion or self-esteem, so there is no greater joy than to be called of God as was Aaron, to receive not only "grace," but "apostleship."

'Now then, dear Andrew, we are ambassadors for Christ, as though God did beseech men by us. We, then, as fellow-workers with God must beseech men not to receive the grace of God in vain. May God count you faithful, putting you into the ministry, and may the arms of your hands be made strong by the hands of the mighty God of Jacob. For a while you were like Moses. It "came into your heart" to be a minister of God's Word to deliver Israel out of Egypt, for you supposed that your brethren would have understood how that by your hand God would deliver souls.

But they understood not, and so you fled to the land of Midian and called your name " Gershom," for you said " I am a stranger here." But when the set time was expired the Angel Jehovah of the Bush that burned, yet was not consumed, has met thee in the wilderness—" and *now*, come, I will send thee into Egypt." Dear Andrew, forgive thy younger brother speaking to thee as if he were an elder—one that must ever sit at thy feet and walk in thy footsteps, following thee in as far as thou followest Christ. God has also visited your friends with sore bereavement, to remind you that it is no permanent connection you are going to form,—that you must have the same faith as Abraham and Isaac and Jacob, who all dwelt in tents in the land of promise, declaring plainly that they seek a country. . . . I hear of your preaching, and am refreshed by the very echo of it. . . . My people have a great attachment to you. . . . I long to know all your feelings. I heard from Mr. Nairne, who says that all the godly people of the country-side are rejoicing. I long to have an open door to preach in these rural retreats. May the Lord appear to you saying, " Fear not, for I am with thee—for I have much people in this parish." Good-bye. May He keep you in perfect peace. Peace upon Israel.—Yours affectionately,   ROBERT MURRAY M'CHEYNE.'

It is interesting to find Mr. M'Cheyne in the same year giving his friend kindly advice about his style of preaching and how to improve it : ' Dear Andrew, study to express yourself very clearly. I sometimes observe obscurity of expression. Form your sentences very regularly. . . . It sometimes strikes me you begin a sentence before you know where you are to end it, or what is to come in at the end.'

Once, when referring to the first sermon he ever preached, Mr. Bonar said, ' In looking over my notes I find I made a great mistake. I had no " heads." When we are young men we are apt to think this is the right way to preach—going straight on from topic to topic ; but the hearers need pegs on which to hang the truth.'

The people were not greatly impressed by his first sermon, and this inclined the old minister the more

in his favour.   Years after an honest man said to Mr.
Bonar, 'It's a gude thing, sir, we didna like ye at first,
or we wadna hae had ye noo!'

The country is one of great natural beauty.   The
village of Collace lies half-hidden among trees and
hedgerows in the rich, level lands of Strathmore.   To
the north the long dark line of the Grampians throws a
distant grandeur over the soft Lowland scenery.   Near
the scattered cottages of the village the square tower of
the parish church peeps out from the trees.   Dunsinnane
House was Mr. Bonar's first home at Collace, and then
he came to the Kirkton, an old-fashioned, ivy-covered
house by the roadside, close to the church.   The garden
was separated from the churchyard only by a wall, and
one day, not long after their arrival, the servant rushed
into the parlour exclaiming, 'Eh, sir, they're buryin' a
bairn at the back door!'   His sister Christian came
with him to this house, and it was a frequent resort
of his mother and the rest of the family.   The Kirkton
is associated with the visits of Robert M'Cheyne, who
often rode over from Dundee to give his services at
Collace.   As he came to the door one wintry day, he
said, 'I have been riding all the way to-day through the
pure white snow, and that verse has been in my mind
all the time, "Wash me, and I shall be whiter than
snow."'   One of his sayings is still remembered in
Collace: 'Bethany was known in Scripture not so much
as Bethany, but as "the town of Mary and her sister
Martha."   I wonder who in this place gives the name
by which it is known in heaven?   It will not be known
there as Collace, but as the town of—perhaps some
bedridden believer up in the hills.'   While preparing
the 'Narrative of a Mission of Inquiry to the Jews,'
Mr. M'Cheyne and Mr. Bonar exchanged work for a
few weeks, that they might have fewer interruptions in

their writing. Some one asked the old minister then how he was getting on with 'that wild man from Dundee'? and his reply was, 'Mr. Bonar is bad enough, but that man is ten times waur!' Of a Sabbath-day during that time Mr. M'Cheyne wrote, 'I preached on "Jesus loved Martha" in the morning. The old minister spoke much on *popular arts, and handling the word of God deceitfully* ; but I did not mind. I preached in the afternoon in the church—nearly quite full—on "Give us of your oil."'

Mr. Bonar's old servant used to tell, years afterwards, of Mr. M'Cheyne's last visit to Collace. He preached in the church, and 'the folk were standin' out to the gate, and the windows were pulled down that those outside might hear. Mr. Cormick (of Kirriemuir) spoke first, and then Mr. M'Cheyne preached on "Lest I myself should be a castaway." I had to come awa' after he began, and I could see from the house the kirk lichted up, and oh, I wearied sair for them to come hame! They stayed at the kirk that nicht till eleven. The folk couldna gi'e ower listenin', and Mr. M'Cheyne couldna gi'e ower speakin'. I mind the time when Mr. Bonar couldna get his tea ta'en for folk comin' and speerin' if conversion was true. Oh, to hear Mr. M'Cheyne at prayers in the mornin'! It was as if he could never gi'e ower, he had sae muckle to ask. Ye would hae thocht the very walls would speak again. He used to rise at six on the Sabbath mornin', and go to bed at twelve at night, for he said he likit to have the whole day alone with God.'

A servant-girl, in a house where he stayed, described him as '*deein*' to hae folk converted.' A minister in the north was so impressed with his daily life of holiness that he said, 'He is the most Jesus-like man I ever met with,' and went to his room to weep. Dr. Candlish remarked to Dr. Moody-Stuart, 'I can't understand M'Cheyne; grace seems to be natural to him.'

One or two of Mr. M'Cheyne's letters to Mr. Bonar, both before and after the settlement of the latter at Collace, are full of interest. One is dated, Dundee, 13th September 1836 :—

'MY DEAR ANDREW,—Your kind letter has just found me, and rejoices me much. I have often, often wished to see your face in this the scene of my labours and trials. Indeed, I need much to be refreshed by you, and I do hope that God will give you not a prosperous journey only, but a full heart, that I who tarry at home may share in the spoil. . . . Oh, to be kept lying in the dust while we work for God! I am often given up to feel the desperate wickedness of my heart, and I believe it is all to keep me in the dust. Now, my dear Andrew, be sure to make out your visit to me and refresh me with your presence. . . . On Thursday evening is my prayer-meeting, which you must join us in. I shall be so happy to get a word from you that will encourage me and my people. On Thursday I will take you round my parish. On Friday I will make you write a sermon, on Saturday commit it, and on Sabbath preach it; and you shall have one from me. Do consent to this if you can, and we shall have another from you in the evening. I must not write any more, as it gets late. It quite lightens me to think you are coming. . . .

'And now farewell. "I have many things to write, but I will not with ink and pen write unto thee. But I trust I shall shortly see thee, and we shall speak face to face. Peace be to thee."—Your faithful friend,   ROBERT MURRAY M'CHEYNE.

'I subjoin a map that you may find the house where I live; it is about five minutes' walk further west than the church—the westmost lane in Dundee going down to the sea.'

Another was written when Mr. Bonar was working as missionary in Edinburgh, without any prospect of being sent to a sphere of labour of his own.

'*19th January* 1838.

'MY DEAR ANDREW,—I am sorry this is Friday night, or I would have written much more at length. Yet a word may convey my kind wishes to you for this year we have begun, and may remind you of your feeble brother in the north, who needs all the encouragement you have to spare—and specially needs to be carried upon your shoulder and on your breast when you are within the veil. I return you your sermon on "Lord, my heart is not haughty." I had no intention of carrying it away with me when I asked it from you, or would have got your leave first. I hope you did not need it. It has been a sweet word to me, and I have often thought of it. My soul is far from being like a weaned child. I sometimes tremble when I think that afflictions will be needful to wean my soul. . . . You would hear that Mr. Reid is to remain at Chapelshade. . . . Dear Andrew, God is keeping you in the hollow of His hand. When a warrior begins to fight, he never throws his best dart at the enemy first. He throws some weak arrows among them, just to begin the contest; he keeps his polished shaft for the hottest of the fight. Your day is coming, or, if you be lifted away from the scene of conflict to the land of peace and triumph, we will both adore the Sovereign Father of our Lord Jesus, who loves some so well that He must have them to minister to Himself in praises rather than in conflicts. I send you your tract on the Jews, of which I have made large use. I last night gave the substance of it to my prayer-meeting, and engaged their interest very much in behalf of the dearly-beloved of God's soul. I quite agree with you in thinking them the first object of all missionary exertion, and hope hereafter to devote more and more of my thoughts and prayers to them. . . . Tell me when you will come over and see me and preach to my people. . . . Do write and tell me the meaning of any parts of the Bible. I am very ignorant, and thirst for knowledge of the Word—but most of Jesus Himself, the true Word. May He abide in you—you in Him.—Yours affectionately,   R. M. M'CHEYNE.'

A letter which shows another side of Mr. M'Cheyne's character, is one which he wrote to his doctor, who had refused to send in a bill for his services. Mr. M'Cheyne enclosed his fee, along with these lines :—

' Dear Doctor, I fear you will think me too merry,
But it strikes me you 're making two bites of a cherry.
You know when a patient won't swallow a pill,
You never consult his sweet mouth or his will,

You say, "Take the physic or you may depend on 't
You 'll never get well, come, drink—there 's an end on 't."
Dear Doctor, allow me to borrow a leaf
From your book of prescriptions, commanding and brief.
" Hoc aurum et papyr," mix—pocket—call " Dust ! "
And swallow it quickly.   Come, Doctor, you must.
I had rather want stipend, want dinner, want tea,
Than my Doctor should ever work wanting his fee.
Forgive this intrusion—and let me remain,
In haste, your affectionate R. M. M'Cheyne.'
                    ' Dulce est desipere in loco.'

Dundee, April 4, 1838.

Mr. M'Cheyne's early death, though regarded as an
irreparable loss to the Church of God, was destined,
through the publication of his *Memoir*, to effect perhaps
a greater work than his prolonged life could have
accomplished.   Mr. Bonar's love for him was touchingly
apparent in his after-life.   The 25th of March was
always remembered as the day on which Robert
M'Cheyne went home.   In 1873 he writes, after a visit
to St. Peter's, Dundee, ' There is still some peculiar
fragrance in the air round Robert M'Cheyne's tomb ! '

When in America in 1881, his thoughts went back to
his friend through all the long years since 1843, when
looking on scenes of which they had often talked together.   He writes :—

Saturday, 20th August 1881.—' How deeply interested would
Robert M'Cheyne have been to-day had he been with us ! he who
used to speak of this place.   It was really strange to me and
wonderful that this morning I should be on the way to Northampton where so much work was done for God in other days.
The day was beautiful, everything bathed in sunshine. . . . We
came to what was the old street where Jonathan Edwards'
house stood. . . . The two great elm-trees in front of the house
are remarkable in themselves.   It was under these the man of
God and his wife used to sit, so that the spot became like the oak
of Mamre, God meeting them there ; and in those days the

ground all round was a grove of pines where Jonathan Edwards used to walk and pray.'

His thoughts were still dwelling on old memories of his friend, when next day he writes again :—

'Filled with alarm and regret in reviewing the Lord's mercies to me, in using me to write the *Memoir of R. M. M'Cheyne*, for which I am continually receiving thanks from ministers. Why was I commissioned to write that book? How poor have been my returns of thankfulness. Oh, when shall I attain to the same holy sweetness and unction, and when shall I reach the deep fellowship with God which he used to manifest?'

The history of the *Memoir of M'Cheyne* would in itself be enough to fill a volume. The wonderful blessing which has everywhere followed its circulation was always attributed by the author to the prayer offered at the time of its publication ; and is also owing, doubtless, to the prayer which has followed its course ever since.

The members of the Deputation to the Jews in 1839, returned into the midst of scenes of revival in their own land. The blessing reached Collace as well as other places, and the pastor's heart rejoiced to find souls seeking Christ in all parts of his parish. There was great depth and reality in the work of grace, deep conviction of sin, and correspondingly clear apprehension of the way of salvation. Many remarkable conversions occurred among old and young. One man who had been a drunkard was brought to the Saviour and became afterwards an elder in the church, and a consistent follower of Christ. On his death-bed he said, 'I am going to the God of the Bible to enjoy Him. I know that my Redeemer liveth.' Another describing his conversion, said, 'Havena I been stoopid, sir? It was sae simple, just as if I had stoopit down and lifted up a clod at my feet.'

A sawyer, who was busy at his work when the light broke upon him, was so filled with joy that he began to preach to his fellow-workman, and had to cry, 'Lord, keep back some o' the licht, for this poor vessel is not able to contain it.' One who was very anxious dreamed that she saw a wide river rolling between her and Christ. She looked and looked at Him on the other side, and as she looked, she suddenly found herself beside Him! She awoke, and saw the meaning of her dream.

A man in the village of Sachar was so terribly awakened, that for many days he was almost ready in his misery to take away his own life. He became a useful member of the church after his conversion, and his frequent prayer at their prayer-meetings used to be 'Wauken them up, Lord, wauken them up!' A very sad case occurred of a man deeply awakened under William Burns' preaching at Dundee, and for days in great agony of mind. After a time all his concern passed away, and he lived and died in indifference.

Coming out of church one Sabbath, Miss Bonar met an old woman weeping, and in great distress of mind. 'Many of the sermons,' she said, 'had grippit her before, but none had grippit her sae sair as this.' She found peace in believing, and along with some others, began a prayer-meeting in the village of Sachar where she lived. A little company of factory girls used to walk seven miles from Stanley to attend the services at Collace. They had to cross the river Tay on their way, and, when they were returning home late one night, the ferryman refused to take them over, so they lay down cheerfully to sleep among the bushes till the morning.

The thirst for the word of God was very great. Not only did the people walk long distances to hear, but they never seemed to grow tired of listening. One evening, Mr. Milne had come from Perth, and Mr.

Manson from the neighbouring village of Abernyte to take part in a meeting at Collace, and it was agreed that each of them should give a short address. Mr. Milne spoke first, and became so interested in his subject—'a well of water springing up to everlasting life'— that he went on for two hours. The people sat motionless, and, quite unconscious of how long he had spoken, he turned to Mr. Manson as he finished, and said, 'Now, brother, you will say a word!'

When Mr. Bonar came to Collace there were perhaps not more than half a dozen living Christians in the place.[1] From those days of revival the parish began to assume a different aspect even outwardly. Few, if any, idlers were to be seen outside the cottage-doors on a Sabbath day, and family worship was conducted morning and evening in nearly every household. 'Drops from heaven fell' on every side, yet still the pastor longed for more. 'Oh that Collace were full of prayer like Kilsyth! Oh that the church were full of people weeping for sin, and oh that there were needing to be psalms sung to drown the weeping of the people as they get a sight of their sins!'

'It is truly encouraging,' he writes to his brother Horatius, 'to hear of souls awakened, and yet it is also alarming that there should be so few,—alarming to ourselves who preach, since we have a promise. I often feel quite certain that my own prayerlessness is the reason why so few of my people are awakened. The thought fills me with pain, and excites me to a new course of prayer.'

---

[1] He used often to quote the old rhyme which before those days was not applicable to Collace :
> 'Truth and grace cam' by Collace,
>   And by the door o' Dron,
> But the coup and the stoup o' Abernyte
>   Mak' mony a merry man.'

'There have been some interesting cases of conversion. But when is the heaven to become black with
clouds and winds, and the rain to fall in a Carmel-
flood?'

'I rejoice with you,' he writes to Mr. Manson, '[at
tidings of revival]. I try my own soul by this test,—can
I be as glad at this news as if my own parish had been
the scene of these wonders?'

He closes a letter asking Mr. Manson to come and
preach, with the words, 'I wish you would bring out
with you the trumpet that awakes the dead.'

Dr. Bonar's memory was full of recollections of the
preachers and preaching of those times. He used to
tell an anecdote of Mr. Burns as an instance of how
God overrules for good what seem to us the mistaken
impulses of his people. He went one day to Perth
to attend a meeting in St. Leonard's, at which Mr.
Burns was to preach. When Mr. Bonar arrived at the
manse, Mr. Burns exclaimed, 'Oh, this is most pro-
vidential. I have a strong impression that I should be
in Dundee to-night. You and Mr. Milne will take this
meeting.' 'But,' they remonstrated, 'you are advertised
to preach here.' 'Oh, you two will do it,' he said, and
left the room, returning bag in hand to say good-bye.
There was nothing for it but that they should go to the
church and conduct the meeting. Mr. Bonar gave the
first address, and Mr. Milne followed. Some days
after, as Mr. Milne was riding to Bridge of Earn, a
woman ran out of her house to speak to him. 'Oh, sir,'
she said, 'I will never forget Monday night. I was
awakened by the first address, and led to Christ by the
second!'

Mr. Burns preached one evening in Sachar, and his
prayer greatly impressed the people. He asked for the
young minister that the Lord would put a sharp sickle

in his hand, that he might gather in many souls to Christ, and for the old minister he prayed, 'Lord, bless the old man who has been so long in this parish. May his flesh come again like that of a little child.'

When Dr. Hamilton was minister in the neighbouring village of Abernyte, a man in his parish used to walk over to Collace to church. He apologised for doing so and said, 'It's because Mr. Bonar is no sae learned as you!' A good woman, who used to worship in Abernyte church in Mr. Manson's time, said to a friend one evening, as they walked home from church to her house at the foot of Dunsinnane Hill, 'I wish I had a memory like Mr. Manson.' 'Toots, woman,' was her friend's reply, 'if you were to be a minister you would have a memory like him, but you're no' a minister, and ye dinna need it!' This woman came to live in Perth in her old age, and, when attending the Conference meetings, Mr. Bonar always went to see her. On the last visit he paid to her, she did not know him, and did not even look up when told some one had come to see her. At last he began to speak, and, at the sound of his voice, she started up exclaiming, 'It's my ain auld minister!' and flung her arms round his neck!

After the Disruption of 1843,[1] the Free Church congregation met for some time in a tent near Kinrossie, and many a remarkable scene was witnessed there. People came from miles round to be present at the Communion services. Long after, Dr. Bonar looked back to those times with peculiar tenderness, and often on the morning of the Summer Communion in Finnieston (held on the same day as in Collace), remembered his old flock in the country. 'Our Communion was very sweet,' he writes in June 1843, 'immense crowds of people.

[1] Some one met the old minister after the Disruption and asked how he was getting on. 'Oh fine,' was his reply, 'opposition's the life of trade!'

About sixty of the St. Peter's people came from Dundee. I have got great comfort in my young communicants. Six of them I believe to be really new creatures in Christ Jesus.'

One who used often to hear him preach in those days, and who afterwards became an elder in his church in Finnieston, Mr. J. H. Dickson, has given some recollections of these Communion services. 'My remembrances of Mr. Bonar's ministry in Collace are mostly connected with Communion seasons. There were no conferences then, but, after the great revival of 1840-41, groups of people used to come from the surrounding districts— not because the gospel was not preached in those places, but the new life which the revival brought, made Christians long for the fellowship of these Communion seasons in Perth, Blairgowrie, and Collace. Great blessing was received, and earnest prayer went up for weeks before such seasons. The one most fixed in my memory was held in June after the Disruption. The congregation met in a large canvas tent. The day was bright and sunny. Mr. Bonar's closing address after the Tables was on Song iv. 6 : "Until the day break, and the shadows flee away." He referred to Mr. M'Cheyne as standing on the " mountain of myrrh " till the day break, and, as he pointed to the bread and wine before him as shadows that would flee away, there came a great hush over the congregation, and then the sound of sobbing from the Dundee people who were present, at the mention of their beloved minister's name. Mr. Bonar himself was much affected ; indeed it was a weeping congregation.' Of other such days Mr. Bonar writes :—

'It was a good day yesterday, brother, especially at eveningtide. Mr. Cormick was very lively and solemn, the Supper itself a time to my own soul when I felt oneness with Jesus. . . . When breezes from Lebanon blow, what a world the eternal world appears, and what a Lord is the Lord of glory!'

'Yesterday I felt a little of "abounding grace," and the blessedness of being sure yet to be holy, holy, holy. It seemed a very short day—"the sun hasted to go down," I thought. We would need a *long* eternity, or heaven would be no heaven, it would be so soon over.'

'I rode up to Blairgowrie to the Lord's Supper. I felt that there the gift of God to sinners, and the heart of God to sinners, is so fully and exclusively set forth that the Lord's Table is really the *stereotyping of the Gospel.*'

After a Communion season an elderly woman, who had lately been converted, said, 'I canna say much, but my heart's like a burnin' coal!'

THE GOOD PASTOR

'Chosen not for good in me,
  Wakened up from wrath to flee,
  Hidden in the Saviour's side,
  By the Spirit sanctified.
  Teach me, Lord, on earth to show,
  By my love, how much I owe.'—*R. M. M'Cheyne.*

CHAPTER II

AMONG the thatched cottages of Kinrossie, with its pretty village green and antique market-cross, stands the Free Church of Collace. Not far distant, on the edge of Dunsinnane wood, is the manse, hidden from view more than it was forty years ago by the growth of trees and hedges. A vine and a fig-tree climb up on either side of the old study window, and over other two windows are carved the Hebrew words, '*He that winneth souls is wise*' and '*For yet a little while, and He that shall come will come and will not tarry.*' The path from the manse through Dunsinnane wood became a spot hallowed by prayer and communion with God. One day a man going along that way heard the sound of voices in the wood, and found Mr. Bonar kneeling there in prayer with two young men. The manse was finished a few months after his marriage in 1848. An old woman in the parish, when Mr. Bonar told her that he was going to be married, remarked with more plainness than politeness, 'Weel, sir, I hope it's a' richt, but we women are awfu' cheats!' This same old woman said of a minister who had come from the other side of the river to preach to them, 'He wasna worth his water-fraucht!' In those days it was no uncommon sight to see one and another in church stand up during the sermon to shake off drowsiness, and sometimes Mrs. Bonar would touch a sleepy hearer with her parasol.

Mr. Bonar thought nothing of preaching twice and then riding several miles in the evening to preach somewhere else, or to visit a sick person. Every Sabbath morning at ten o'clock he conducted a Bible class for young men and women, which was attended with much blessing, and was the means of stirring up many to search the Scriptures, and of leading them to Jesus, the Way, the Truth, and the Life. An old woman, who had learned to love God's Word, said to Mr. Bonar, ' I wonder how God's people get through the Bible, for I am often stopped a whole day at one verse.' A young woman said to him, ' I often wanted to die after I found Christ, for I was afraid of sinning. But one day I remembered Christ's words : " I pray not that Thou shouldst take them out of the world, but that Thou shouldst keep them from the evil that is in the world ; " and I don't want to die now.' The experience of another was very peculiar. She was so sorely tried by the Tempter that she went out into the fields alone, hoping to get rid of his evil suggestions. But Satan followed her and told her that the Old Testament was not true. She turned to the New Testament, but he said that was not true either. When she came as far as the Metre Psalms he told her *they* were not true, but she got a little rest at the paraphrase : ' Behold the Saviour on the Cross.' At another time the devil tried to persuade her that there was no God, and that she had no soul. When tempted at last to disbelieve everything, she sat down and told him that the places mentioned in the Bible were real, for Mr. Bonar had seen them when he was in Palestine. But the Tempter said, ' Mr. Bonar is a liar!'

Many interesting incidents occurred in connection with his visitation. He went to see an old bed-ridden man who reminded him of a sermon he had preached ten years before. ' I mind,' the old man said, ' you spoke about the Cave of Adullam. "Do you like the Cave, and do you like the Captain? Then come in— come in—no other condition." My, *it sank into my heart like oil.*' He asked a boy to hold his horse one day, while he went into a cottage. As he was re-mounting, and putting his foot in the stirrup, he turned to the lad and said, 'Do you ever think you have a soul?' The question was never forgotten. Coming home one night from a meeting at Rait, he lost his way, and as he wandered about he said to himself, 'Can I give thanks for this?' In a short time he came to a house, and was just going to the door to ask direction for his way home, when a girl came out and exclaimed, 'Mr. Bonar! you 're the very person I want to see.' He found she was in great distress of mind, and was able to give thanks that, in losing his way among the hills, he had been led to find a soul. Returning home late one night from a meeting, he heard of the serious illness of one who had been formerly in his service, and at once had his pony saddled, and rode three miles to see him. After this he continued his visits every day till he recovered. He fixed a certain night for calling on a young married couple, when he was likely to find them both at home. The night came, and with it a storm of wind and rain. They said to each other, 'There will be no minister here to-night,' but, true to his word, the minister appeared at the hour appointed.

One winter evening, when walking to Scone to preach, he overtook a woman on the road, and began to talk to her, giving her a tract when they parted. Some time after, he noticed a widow in church, who waited after service was over, and said to him, 'I am the woman you spoke to that dark night on the road to Scone and never saw. You gave me a tract. My son at home, long ill, had been troubled about himself, and that tract was the very one for him, and brought light to his soul. He made me come over from Kinnaird to tell you.'

It was his habit in the country to rise at six o'clock in the summer mornings, and seven o'clock in winter. 'You'll be thrashin' your strae the nicht, sir,' was the remark of one of his people on a Saturday evening, for, even then, Saturday was carefully set apart for prayer and preparation for the Lord's Day. His sermons were not always fully written out, and in the pulpit he only used little pieces of paper on which the 'heads' were jotted down in shorthand. When preaching one day in the tent at Kinrossie, a puff of wind blew away his notes, and the people had such a horror of sermon-reading that nobody would lift them up. It is needless to say the minister continued his sermon without them.[1]

Mrs. Bonar's letters and his own give bright little glimpses of their life at Collace. Three children were born in the manse, and, until after their removal to Glasgow, death did not cast its shadow over their home. The first Sabbath in church after his marriage Mr. Bonar gave out these lines of the Sixteenth Psalm to be sung :—

> ' Unto me happily the lines
> In pleasant places fell ;
> Yea, the inheritance I got
> In beauty doth excel.'

His quiet humour showed itself in various ways. A good man in the parish maintained that, because he and his wife were believers, their children would be born without sin. Mr. Bonar tried to reason with him, and

---

[1] As Moderator of the Free Church General Assembly in 1878 he read his opening address with the greatest difficulty. This was the only time he was known to read a sermon or address.

then said in his quiet way, 'Wait and see!' When his child was a few months old the man came back to him and said, 'I see, sir, you were quite right!' His description of a brother - minister, who had not his own bright hopefulness, was, '—— is like one of the Emmaus disciples : " he walks *and is sad*."' One of his elders used to recall his visits with him to a neighbouring farm, where he went to hold a meeting in the evening. The road was full of ruts and holes, and sometimes Mr. Bonar would be standing in mud up to the ankles, laughing and making fun of his droll appearance. In one of his letters to Mrs. Bonar from Collace, he says:—

'I am enjoying myself to-night by the fireside alone, for it is very cold. Nothing new to tell you. . . . Our people think " Mr. John (Dr. Bonar of Greenock) was uncommon lively " this time. . . . I happened to meet L. P. at her door to-day. She has been "complaining," and here is her account of herself : " You see I pu'ed neeps when they were frosty without my gloves, and so the cauld grippit my two hands, and spilt all the bluid, and raised the influenza."'

Another time he writes to Mrs. Bonar in Edinburgh :—

'A taste of solitude helps to make you and anything of yours more prized than ever. The cuckoo is sending his note through the woods now, and the young grass is appearing. Part of the walks are gravelled. The corn is breering.[1] . . . Watch (the dog) has imitated you—that is, he is away seeing his friends. . . . Take a farewell look at Minto Street for me ; I'll never forget it—the houses down to No. 49[2] are all familiar to me, and your green before the door, and the rooms where we used to sit. If we get so fond of an earthly abode, what shall we feel to a mansion in the Heavens, or to a place in the New Earth where no decay shall ever enter ? Meanwhile, live on Him who is " the same yesterday, to-day, and for ever." Take this as your text, and think on it all the time of the flitting.'

---

[1] Appearing above ground.

[2] Mrs. Bonar's home in Edinburgh where her marriage took place, April 4th, 1848.

During one of his visits to Ireland, before his marriage, in very stormy weather, he wrote the following little allegory and sent it to 49 Minto Street :—

'There was a pilgrim whose lot it was to cross the sea and go up and down the land of Israel. He had been in many perils by sea and by land, from robbers and from burning heat, and yet was no way injured. He could still sing, "O that men would praise the Lord for His goodness." He sat down one day, and, no doubt thinking of the storms that often toss the little boats on the Lake of Galilee, he told the following story:

THE STORY

'I knew a daughter of Zion who feared the Lord and trusted with all her heart in His grace. She had herself been brought through a land of deserts and of pits, and never had found Him a wilderness. She read and believed the words written in Matt. vi. 25-34, which Levi the son of Alpheus was commanded to write by the Holy Ghost. But still, through temptation and a fearful heart, she often forgot *the Person who spoke those words* : and always in such seasons care arose in her soul. One dark night there arose a strong wind; it tore down the boughs of aged trees, it raised the waves of the sea to a great height, it shook many dwellings, and it roared loudly over all. This godly daughter of Zion heard it, and her heart grew fearful in behalf of one for whom she often prayed, and who loved and prayed for her. No doubt she believed that her God cared for him, and that not a hair of his head could fall without our Father; but still she feared and was very "careful." She imagined him to be on the sea, very pale and sick, the ship heaving on the waves, and its planks creaking as if they would break, the sky dark, the rain falling in torrents. There was nothing sad, but she thought it possible. In this state of mind she could not praise the Lord, her harp lay unstrung. She could not pray; she had no sweet meditation. Nay, her body was worn out with sleeplessness and care.

'Morning came, the sun shone peacefully all around. A messenger arrived. She heard that the object of her care had never set foot on the ship, but had spent, and was to spend, some days on land in more than usual rest. Upon this she began to remember Ps. cxxvii. 2, and said to her soul reproachfully, "Alas, I might have all that time been engaged in better thoughts! I might have prayed, praised, and exercised faith in the care of my High Priest. Even my body might have been the better of this, as well as my soul." From that day forth (says the pilgrim who tells the story, and who often to this day thinks upon that daughter of Zion) she learned to be less anxious, I trust, and to be more satisfied with *the Lord's knowing how to keep His own*, whether *she* knows or not.'

'A good story for next *Christian Treasury*, and a good motto would be Luther's words to Philip Melanchthon : "Philip must be told to cease from the attempt of *being himself the ruler of the world*." '

Mrs. Bonar, when Isabella Dickson, was brought to Christ during the times of revival in Edinburgh in 1842. Along with her friend, Miss Gifford (afterwards the wife of Dr. Alex. Raleigh), she attended a prayer-meeting for the Jews, held in St. Andrew's Church. Mr. M'Cheyne spoke at this meeting, and what he said interested her, but it was the impression of his personal holiness, rather than his words, that most deeply affected her. 'There was something singularly attractive about Mr. M'Cheyne's holiness,' she told her husband afterwards. 'It was not his matter nor his manner either that struck me ; it was just the *living epistle of Christ*— a picture so lovely, I felt I would have given all the world to be as he was, but knew all the time I was dead in sins.' On reading a letter in the last chapter of *M'Cheyne's Memoir*, from one who had been impressed in a similar way, she felt startled, it was so like her own experience. Mr. Bonar's acquaintance with her began during the long and trying illness of her mother, whom she nursed with unwearied devotion till her death in 1847. During this sad time the Twenty-third Psalm was her never-failing resort. She once said, in reference to it, 'O, if you only knew all that I have got by it! Sometimes when they sing it in church it is too much for me. I don't know what I would have done without it and

the orphan's verse, Psalm xxvii. 10.' When, years after
his beloved wife's pilgrimage was over, her husband lay
down to rest at the end of his long life-journey, the
words of the Twenty-third Psalm, sung by his dying bed,
calmed the hearts of his children as they watched his
gentle passage through the valley of the shadow of death
into the Father's house beyond.

Often during those eighteen years of seclusion Mr.
Bonar wondered what might await him in the future,
and if his work might not some day lie in a wider field.
Several invitations came to him from other places, but
he did not see God's call in any of them. It needed
a very clear indication of His will to make him think
of leaving his beloved flock. While in London at
one time, he wrote to his brother-in-law, Mr. William
Dickson :—

'Many an upbraiding do I meet with for what they count the
"folly and absurdity" of continuing to feed a few sheep at Collace,
rather than agree to plunge into the mass of misery among souls
here. But, nevertheless, I am not moved from my belief that the
Lord may mean to work more in a very small spot than in a great
city, while, at the same time, He may use country shepherds to go
up now and then to the city, and tell what things the Lord has
made known to them.'

In regard to a definite call to London, he wrote :—

'As to London, I shall be slow to move in such a matter. I
sometimes think that Satan may occasionally try in such ways to
extrude a minister—it is not always the moving of the cloudy
pillar.'

When his removal to Glasgow began to be seriously
talked of, he wrote to one of his friends :—

'I am much pressed to consider the subject of Glasgow evangeli-
sation—in short, to agree to be called to a district and church
about to be erected in Finnieston in Glasgow. I have prayed,
considered, and in every way reviewed the matter as impartially

as I could, and the result is I am feeling my way toward it. The thousands in that part of Glasgow (it is quite like a district of London) made me yearn ; so few to care for them, and every day more houses built, and more souls arriving, richer and poorer. What think you? To leave Collace I have always thought would be like Abraham leaving Ur of the Chaldees—that is, nothing but the clear call of the God of glory would effect it ; but this seems to me like His call.'

The affection which united minister and people was often touchingly manifested after their separation, as well as during their long intercourse. It is more than thirty years since the pillar-cloud led him away from Collace on another stage of his journey heavenward, but his memory is lovingly cherished by those who still remain, and he is mourned for as if he had left them but yesterday.

'Little as I am acquainted with the Lord, I will leave it as my testimony that there is none like Him. God has been good to a soul that but poorly sought Him. Often, on riding home on Sabbath evenings, I have felt "Whom have I in heaven but Thee? and there is none upon earth that I desire besides Thee. . . .' Believer, is He not all this to you? O sinner, O unsaved ones of my flock, He might be more than all this to you! Young people, whom I greatly long for, remember what James Laing[1] said to one, 'Remember, if I see you at the left hand, I told you to come to Christ.' Shall I see any of these faces on which I have so often looked, and those which have so oft looked up to me, on the left hand? Shall any one here gaze on an angry Judge? any hear Him say, Depart? I beseech you, receive Christ . . . to-day. I beseech you, by remembrance of past Sabbaths, by the many witnesses that the Lord sent among you from time to time, by the messages of

[1] *The Lily Gathered*, by Rev. R. M. M'Cheyne.

grace so many and so varied, by the joy that your salva-
tation would give above as well as here and to yourselves, by the thought of approaching death, by the
thought of the Lord's speedy coming, by the opening of
yonder veil, when eternity shall receive you, and time
be for ever gone, receive Christ now.' [1]

[1] Mr. Bonar's Farewell Sermon at Collace, preached on the 19th of
October 1856.

IN THE CITY

'When God comes to a man He does not only say " Arise, receive !" but " Arise, shine !" '—*A. A. B.*

CHAPTER III

IT was on a dreary December day in 1856 that the first congregation assembled in Finnieston Free Church, Glasgow, for the induction of the minister. He is described as being at that time a 'tall, straight, and somewhat spare man, about forty-five years of age, with hair just tinged with grey.' The addresses were long, and one of the members of Presbytery on the platform made a sign to him to sit down, and even pushed a chair forward with his foot ; but he remained standing. The incident was a trivial one, but to those who knew him it was characteristic. Ten or twelve people formed the nucleus of the congregation, and three elders from Free St. Matthew's Church kindly gave their help to the new Territorial Mission Church, until it was able to stand by itself. One of these elders, Mr. Andrew Nielson, remained in the congregation, and became one of its best and truest helpers.

The attendance on the first Sabbath was large, but for many a day after there was only a sprinkling of people in the church. The district round was closely populated, and circumstances altogether combined to make Dr. Bonar feel 'like a missionary to the heathen, who has to spend months in learning the language and habits of the people.' . . . 'I must be content gradually to get acquainted with the faces and characters and the ways of my poor district, and to seek openings among the indifferent, the drunken, the lazy, the ignorant, the practical atheists, the bitter Papists, the formal professors, the young and old, sick and healthy.'

'I have plenty of work, but few Jacobs are finding the ladder between heaven and earth. Most sleep on, and then journey on to eternity with their staff in hand, and nothing more—little comfort on earth, and none at all beyond earth. O for the Spirit's outpouring!'

The devoted teacher of Grace Street School had been carrying on work in the district before the church was built, and many others—office-bearers, tract-distributors, Sabbath-school teachers—now added their help. At the close of 1857 the roll of communicants was 136, and the usual attendance at church from 400 to 500. Dr. Bonar used to recall the first inquirer who came to his house—a young woman dressed in deep mourning, and in great distress. He asked her if she had met with some bereavement lately. She replied, 'Yes, I have lost a brother, but I am not mourning so much for him, but that I can't find my Saviour.' It was two years before the work really began to tell on the neighbourhood; then the wave of the American revival swept over Scotland and touched Finnieston, and days of blessing followed. A gentleman one day asked, 'How are things doing with you? How are you getting on?' 'Oh, we are looking for great things,' was Dr. Bonar's reply. 'You must not expect too much,' said his friend. 'We can never hope for too much,' he responded. He sowed the seed unweariedly, and always in hope, carrying the word of life into the lanes and dark closes, day after day, and week after week. Some who remember those days speak of him as being then in his fullest vigour of mind and body. Nobody escaped his notice, and his quickness in recognising faces was remarkable.

Not unfrequently he was asked by Roman Catholics in the district to perform the marriage ceremony for them. He always accepted these invitations, for they gave him an opportunity of setting forth the simple gospel to the company—mostly Roman Catholics—who assembled on the occasion. He was invariably well received, and welcomed with the words, 'Come along, yer Riverence!'

The first meeting of workers in the congregation numbered only twelve. Long after, in reviewing the past, Dr. Bonar referred to their small beginnings and said, ' We can say with Jacob, With our staff we passed over Jordan, and the Lord very soon made us two bands. We will hear a great deal in the day of the Lord of how the workers found the lost pieces of silver.' He used to say about different methods of work, ' There is more originality in a full heart than in anything else.' At one of the yearly workers' meetings, which became so memorable in the history of the congregation, he spoke specially to visitors and collectors, quoting Isaiah xxxii. 20, ' Blessed are ye that sow beside all waters,' etc. ' You know that the ox is the symbol of laborious strength, and the ass is not a little remarkable for its stubbornness. If you would be persevering and successful in your work, including as it does among other things such weary climbing of stairs, you will have need of this strength of the ox, and this patient stubbornness of the ass!' When reminding collectors of their opportunities of speaking a word for the Master as they went from house to house, he said, ' God blesses those who do more than they are required to do.' At a workers' meeting in later times he read 1 Corinthians xvi. 16, ' Submitting yourselves one to another '—' accommodating yourselves—specially *singers*—falling in with other people's ways of working. We are not to look for thanks from men. Christ says if we do we are no better than the publicans.' ' If you say your hands are full, it is just what they ought to be ! '

' I never like to hear any one say, " I never trouble others with my religion." A believer *must* trouble others with his religion.'

' If you shine as lights now, and cast your light on the shadows around you, you will hear of it in the ages to come. If you do not, God will get others to do it.'

' I have come to believe this to be almost invariably true, that seldom is anything good proposed to us but we have something to object to in it at first. This seems to be the reason for the expression used by our Lord—" Thrust forth labourers." We are all unwilling to go. The truth is, we are all a little lazy. We need to be " thrust forth." '

' Remember,' he said, ' the Lord never uses angels to preach the gospel. It must be sinners that tell sinners what it is that takes away sin. God sends His people, —" You know every bush in which the sheep hide—go you and seek for them." God knew what a wrench it would be for Philip to leave the great awakening in Samaria and go to meet *one* soul in the wilderness ; so He sent His angel to tell him to go. It was as if Christ said to him, " *I* left the ninety-and-nine in the wilderness, to go to seek the one lost sheep. Go *you* and find that lost one in the desert." '

' " Without Me ye can do nothing." Christ has willed that the world should be influenced through the instrumentality of the Christian ; so that, as we say, Without Him *we* can do nothing, He, as it were, says, Without you *I* can do nothing, as if He needed our services.'

' You said you had no time,' he writes to a brother minister. ' Have you not time for all *duty*, and this was a *duty* ? '

It was not the minister's fault if any of his people stood idle in the vineyard. If a stranger came from the country to join Finnieston Church, Dr. Bonar's common practice was to take him with him to the Bible class, then to see the Sabbath-school in Grace Street, and generally, before many days had passed, he found himself installed as a Sabbath-school teacher or a district visitor, or in some way a helper in the work of the congregation. 'The way to rise high in Christ's kingdom is to serve much;' and he carried out this axiom in his own life, and taught others the secret of the same blessedness.

'Lengthened life should be lengthened work.'

'Some good men are very peremptory in asking God to give them souls. That may not be the best service you can do for God. The best service you can give Him is *to submit to His will.*'

'The best part of all Christian work is that part which only God sees.'

'Service for the Master that everybody praises is very dangerous service. Perhaps in the day the Master returns the name of one we never heard of in the Church of Christ may be the highest, because he did most, simply for the Master.'

To those who were prevented from doing active work, but were serving God amid the small duties of daily life, he used to say, 'Remember, there is a reward for "thinking upon His name" (Mal. iii. 16). That is a quiet way of doing good, and open to every one.'

'We are to be rewarded, not only for work done, but for burdens borne; and I am not sure but that the brightest rewards will be for those who bore burdens without murmuring.'

'Burdens are part of a believer's education.'

'Self-forgetting work is heavenly work.'

'Christ's obedience was His taking up our undone work.'

A friend wrote to him, telling him that he felt discouraged in his work. He replied, not by letter, but by a parable:

'While tunnelling the Alps, one of the workmen began one day to think upon his arm, and to speculate on its feebleness. Comparing it with the greatness of the work to be done, he forthwith sat down, sad and depressed. "Stronger men are needed here. Who am I to bore through Mont Cenis?" He uttered this moan aloud, and a voice was heard, a voice from one who was watching over the work and the workmen. The voice said kindly, but at the same time half upbraiding, "Did I not know what your arm could do, and what it could not do, when I sent you to propel, by careful attention to your steam apparatus, that wedge of steel? Think of that little wedge of steel *tipped with diamond.* Why moan over your feeble arm?" A friend of yours, Jeremiah of Anathoth, was asked to carry God's message to a people whom he thought he could in no ways impress, and so he wished to refuse, saying, "Ah, Lord God, I cannot speak, for I am a child (נַעַר)." "Very well," replied the speaker, "a mere boy can carry a message. Go on— go at once. *I am with thee.* I will make thee an iron pillar and brazen wall against the whole land." Up, up at once, and forget your feebleness. *Think of Him whose power accomplishes the mighty work*, and how He asks you simply to see that the wedge of diamond-tipped steel be in its right place.'

'God can do anything,' he said, 'by or for a man in Christ.' A minister, who was having a time of revival in his country congregation, expressed a wish that some of his city brethren would come and help him. Dr. Bonar said quietly, 'I thought you said the Master was with you. Why do you want any of us?'

Every Sabbath was a time of labour from morning to evening, but, though not outwardly a day of rest, it was to him ever 'a delight.' Beginning at half-past ten with the Elders' Prayer-Meeting in the vestry, his labours went on till nine o'clock at night. Sometimes he left home earlier in the morning, hoping to find some one at that hour whom he might induce to go to church or to the Bible-class. Besides conducting the two regular services, he generally went into the little prayer-meeting held during the interval of worship in the session-house. On the day on which the church was opened, a band of godly people were present from Jordanhill, near Glasgow, and met together to wait for the afternoon service. The only place they found in which to wait was beside the stove of the church, and there they gathered to spend the hour in prayer. This was the beginning of a prayer-meeting which has ever since been continued. At half-past five the young men's Bible-class was held, and when that was over, and a visit paid to the Sabbath-school, there was always an evening service in church or mission-hall. He was fond of open-air preaching, and sometimes preached from the steps of the church to a crowd reaching to the other side of the street. It was not without many regrets that the church in Finnieston Street was abandoned, in 1878, for a larger and more commodious place of worship near the West End Park. Uncomfortable and badly ventilated as it was, the old church had many hallowed associations, and more than one could point to a seat in one corner or other, and say, 'I was born there.' Even the old bell had a mission of its own, calling in careless dwellers in the streets around to hear the words of life and salvation. Over the door of the new church are carved the three Hebrew words, חֲכַם נְפָשׁוֹת לֹקֵחַ 'He that winneth souls is wise.' They were put there as an indication of the object of the church's existence, and also in the hope that some Jews passing by might see them, and come in to worship the God of Abraham. Dr. Bonar preached from these words on the day on which the church was opened, explaining

that 'winning' was the word used to describe a hunter
stalking game, and reminding 'soul-winners' that their
work must be done in a wise way. 'How carefully
David prepared to meet Goliath! He chose five
smooth stones out of the brook. He did not assume
that one would be lying to his hand when he needed it.
Never go to the Lord's work with meagre preparation.'

At the close of that day's service he referred to the
comfortable place in which they were now met, and
said, 'We read in the New Testament that our Lord
made the five thousand sit down "because there was
much grass in the place." That is why we have provided cushions in the pews. We believe the Lord Jesus
is not indifferent to your comfort.'

In connection with the new church an incident occurred
which he always referred to with deep thankfulness to
God and gratitude to his friends. The cost was very
much greater than had been anticipated, and the debt
which for some time rested on it was a cause of grave
anxiety to the congregation. Many suggestions were
made as to how it was to be cleared off, and among
other things a bazaar was proposed, of which he strongly
disapproved. He suggested delay as to further plans
until the matter had been made a subject of special
prayer. A full meeting of elders and deacons was
called, and the time was spent in earnest prayer for
God's guidance. About a fortnight afterwards, one of
his elders called upon him one morning. He was busy
in his study, and looking more than usually bright. ' I
have something to show you this morning,' he said, and
taking a letter from his pocket, he added, 'Here is our
bazaar! This contains a cheque for £1000. The Lord
has heard and answered our prayers.'

This gift was sent by friends of Dr. Bonar's, and
transmitted to him by Dr. J. H. Wilson of the Barclay

Church, Edinburgh, who had been the originator of this generous scheme for lightening the burden which lay upon both minister and people. In sending it he wrote to Dr. Bonar:—

'I only wish I could convey to you the expressions of grateful and affectionate regard with which the letters abound ; and while the object is not a personal, but a congregational one, I need not say that it is on purely personal grounds that the whole thing has been done, in the belief that it would be a small contribution to your comfort and freedom in working, in having this burden somewhat lessened.'

Dr. Bonar wrote in reply :—

'*Glasgow*, 15*th January* 1881.

'MY DEAR DR. WILSON,—"It is more blessed to give than to receive"—may this blessedness be yours ! I cannot tell you how this most brotherly act of kindness surprised me and filled me with thankfulness. You could not have done a kinder thing to myself, as well as to my people, for this debt has been of late a most serious burden, and a hindrance to efforts in various directions. And let me mention that it cannot but have an effect on us spiritually ; for it is the answer to special prayer begun. I strongly opposed the scheme of a bazaar when one or two of our Deacons' Court proposed it, and we at last agreed to set apart an evening for prayer on the whole matter. On the appointed evening we had a very good attendance of elders and deacons, and the prayers were fervent and hopeful. And then, we, as a Court, set ourselves to form a scheme which, in the course of a good many years would, if successful, leave us entirely free. This most unexpected and generous gift will wonderfully stimulate our efforts. We do heartily thank the disinterested friends who have taken part in this movement, and will use the words of Ezra, "Blessed be the Lord God of our fathers which hath put such a thing as this into thine heart."

'Meanwhile, reminding yourself, Colonel Young, and all the other unknown friends, of Matt. x. 42 and Heb. vi. 10,—Believe me, dear brother, yours affectionately and gratefully,

'ANDREW A. BONAR.'

There was much pleasant intercourse between the minister and his co-workers. The office-bearers have happy recollections in early years, of evenings when they used to convoy him home from the meetings to his house in St. Vincent Crescent.   Many a helpful talk they had as they walked along, till they reached the door, where they still stood chatting together till Mrs. Bonar's quick ear caught the sound of voices, and she came out to welcome her husband home.   It was at such times that he poured out one incident after another of his work and rich experience, often conveying a deep lesson, and in some cases a lifelong impulse to those who listened.

He took a loving interest in all parts of the work of the church, and his sympathy smoothed away many difficulties.   He would slip quietly into one of the little kitchen-meetings, taking his seat among the hearers, then rising to give a word of cheer and encouragement at the close.   His presence in a meeting acted at all times like a charm.   As he came in, overflowing with brightness and kindliness, his progress, as he went from one to another shaking hands, could be traced by the ripple of light that passed over every face.   Not unfrequently at a tea-meeting or social gathering, the opening was delayed, and the explanation given, 'The minister has not finished shaking hands with the people yet!'

He once told as an illustration of the words in Heb. x. 24: 'Let us consider one another,' etc., an experience of his own when in the country.   There was one man who always sat in the front seat in the gallery, and kept his eye fixed on the minister as if to help him on. If he said anything this good man liked very much, he would look at him with an expression which said 'That's good! come on!' and it cheered the preacher's heart.   He thought this was an example of 'provoking to love and good works.'

His readiness to learn from others was very remarkable, and he had the faculty of drawing out what was best in every one. 'A true disciple,' he said, 'is always learning. Every believer we meet with has something for us if we could only get it. We are wrong if we are not trying to draw out of others what God has given them. Never think you can be of no use to another disciple. God does not give everything to one. Aquila and Priscilla could do a good deal even for Apollos.'

At a meeting in the church one evening, two good men had spoken who were rough and uneducated. Dr. Bonar listened to them with evident enjoyment, and when some one spoke of it to him afterwards, he said, 'If you are very thirsty you will not be particular about the dish you drink out of.'

The work of the Holy Spirit went on silently from week to week, making the ordinary services wells of salvation to thirsting souls. Every Sabbath, to use an expression of his own, there 'was more joy even in happy Heaven, because lost ones were being found.' Each time of revival in Glasgow left its impress more or less on Finnieston. Dr. Bonar did not always approve of all the methods employed by those who were sent to carry on the work, but that did not hinder him from identifying himself with any such movement. He believed God could work even where there might be much imperfection, and he and his people were never left unrefreshed when heavenly showers were falling. The revival under Mr. D. L. Moody in 1873-74 was a marked period in his city ministry. He threw himself into it with his whole heart, helping and sympathising in every possible way. In no congregation were the results of the work more apparent than in Finnieston, and never was the pastor's heart more full of joy. One instance among many others of the Lord's presence at these times, occurred after Mr. Moody's visit to Glasgow when services were continued in Finnieston Church. As Dr. Bonar came into one of these meetings after it had begun, he walked to the front of the platform, and, laying his hand on the rail, he said, 'I feel the breath of the Holy Spirit in this place to-night.' The words, and the solemn way in which they were uttered, were the means of awakening a young woman who was present.

The news of 'a sound of abundance of rain' in any part of the world, specially in the mission field, Jewish or heathen, gladdened his heart, and made him long to hear the same 'joyful sound' at home. When writing to Dr. J. H. Wilson, in 1859, he says :—

'You will have heard of the good news from our Jewish school in Constantinople—ten in one week brought to Christ's feet. I hear, too, of some real work in Aberdeen. The Lord is coming near us. I feel often like Isa. xxiv. 16, on which I was preaching lately. When news comes of "glory to the Righteous One" elsewhere, it goes through my heart with something like a chill, and makes me cry "My leanness! my leanness! Woe unto me!"'

When news came of revival work in the fishing-villages, he used to say, 'The Lord Jesus has still a warm heart to the fishermen!'

'Tell it everywhere,' was his advice on hearing of blessing in any place, 'that is the way to spread it.'

ECHOES OF SPOKEN WORDS

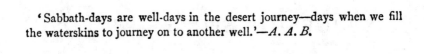

'Sabbath-days are well-days in the desert journey—days when we fill the waterskins to journey on to another well.'—*A. A. B.*

CHAPTER IV

THE congregation that gathered round Dr. Bonar in Finnieston Church was attracted, not by the eloquence of the preaching,[1] but by its simplicity, and the fresh light the preacher threw upon the Scriptures, making them appear to many like a new book. Strangers had to grow accustomed to the peculiarities of his voice, and his habit of letting it suddenly drop just when the hearer's attention was fixed. A good lady in his congregation once remonstrated with him about this, and told him how provoking it was to his hearers to lose some of his very best things. 'How do you know they are the best, if you don't hear them?' was his retort. He liked to tell of a worthy couple who joined his church and told him where their seat was. The woman said, 'I hear you quite well, but he (meaning her husband) says he does not ; but *I* say, *are ye sure ye attend?*' The most ignorant among his hearers could understand his simple unfolding of truth, while many a striking saying fell from his lips as he leaned in his characteristic way over the pulpit, and talked quietly to those before him. The most fearful felt their faith strengthened by his joyous confidence in the things of which he spoke. Eternal things came very near, and unseen things became real, as they listened to one who spoke as if already among them.

[1] 'You know I am no speaker—only a talker,' he says in a letter to a friend.

'Suppose that I, a sinner, be walking along yon golden street, passing by one angel after another. I can hear them say, as I pass through their ranks, " A sinner! a crimson sinner!" Should my feet totter? Should my eye grow dim? No; I can say to them, "Yes, a sinner—a crimson sinner, but a sinner brought near by a forsaken Saviour, and now a sinner who has boldness to enter into the Holiest through the blood of Christ."'

'When Jesus tells us of the glory and beauty of the New Jerusalem,—lest we should think it incredible that feet like ours should ever tread the golden streets, or hands like ours ever pluck the fruit of the Tree of Life, or lips like ours ever taste the water of that pure river,— He says, "John, write: These sayings are *faithful and true.*"'

'If you ask me "What is glory?" well, I can't tell you, but I know that it is a hundred times better than grace.'

'We are like children trying the strings of the harp which we expect yet to use.'

'Never be offended at Christ's providences. He will recompense all to you, even in this life. O believer, *keep Him to His promise!*'

'"The Lord is my Shepherd, I shall not want." Then you have everything but heaven!'

'We have more to do with the world to come than with this world.'

'The nearer you come to Him the better, for you will then be further from the world, and the world will have least power over you.'

'"No man could learn that song,' etc. (Rev. xv. 3). Because there is something in each one's experience that another cannot borrow.'

'What a happy thing it is that it is the " kingdom of

God our Saviour" (2 Peter i. 2). We know *Him* so
well. It was He who put our robe of righteousness on
us. We would be lonely in the great company if we
did not know Him so well. Would it not be a great
comfort to the dying thief that Christ said, "To-day,
. . . *with Me* in Paradise!"'

One Sabbath, when preaching on the image of God
being restored, and the time when 'we shall be like
Him, for we shall see Him as He is,' he suddenly
exclaimed, 'O my people, you won't know your minister
on that day!'[1] 'It will be ecstasy,' he said at another
time, 'to have made this attainment—to love the Lord
our God with all our heart, and soul, and strength, and
mind.' To those to whom that time seemed very far
off, and to whom the trials and difficulties in the way
were very great, he would point out the strength and the
sufficiency of His grace who had promised to complete
the good work He had begun.

'Faith keeps us, but God keeps our faith.'

'If the Father has the kingdom ready for us, He will
take care of us on the way.'

'God will not give us an easy journey to the Promised Land, but He will give us a safe one.'

'We do not need new swords, new spears, new arms.
We only need more eye-salve to see Who is on our side.'

'Jesus left His disciples in the little boat on the Lake
of Galilee purposely, that He might come to them in
the fourth watch of the night and deliver them. I
think He would have come to them sooner—perhaps
in the first or second watch—*if they had trusted Him.*'

[1] A stranger—a young careless girl—sitting in his church one Sabbath,
smiled as he suddenly and seemingly irrelevantly exclaimed, 'Come,
blessed resurrection morn!' In after years the words, in the very tones
in which they were uttered, came to her over and over again with such
power that she marvelled at God's mercy in using what had only excited
her ridicule at the time, to quicken and refresh her on her dying bed.

'None of God's pilgrims fall by the roadside.'

'It is the mark of every quickened soul,' he used to say, 'that he feels his heart going *upward*, as, after His resurrection, Christ would be thinking of *going home.*'

'If you have not *two* heavens, you will never have *one*. If you have not a heaven *here*, you will never have one *yonder.*'

'Judah had a rich land for his inheritance, but Levi had a rich God.'

'Lot would not give up Christ, but he would not give up much *for* Christ.'

'"The world" is all that is outside of the soul's spiritual life.'

'The world is so blind that it did not see the Light of the World when He came. How, then, can you expect that it will see His people?'

When preaching in Collace Church in 1842 he reminded his people of the many offers of salvation they had had during four years of faithful ministry, and said to them, 'These walls are a witness, and their lingering echoes will be witness when I am in the grave. Angels have seen the cup of life held out from this pulpit and put to your lips.'

The same faithful earnestness characterised his preaching at all times, and made his declaration of the love of God in Christ peculiarly sweet and persuasive.

'O men and brethren, look at that Cross, and listen to what it says: "He that hath the Son hath life." I often think, when the Lord is thus pressing you to accept Christ, He has not only stood at the door and knocked, but He has, as it were, opened the door a little to try to persuade you.'

'"Weep not for Me, weep for yourselves and for your children." It is so like Christ to dry up other people's tears, and let His own flow.'

'The Lord left our Saviour in the grave three days that no one might dispute the reality of His death—that there might be time, as it were, to count the pieces of the Ransom-money. When His disembodied spirit was in Paradise these three days, it was like uttering "Finished! Finished! Finished!" over the hills of Paradise.'

'We are asked to accept this salvation—to let this love into our heart, without shedding a single tear, unless it be a tear of love and gratitude.'

'Look into the Fountain, and the very looking will make you thirsty.'

'Take the water of life "freely," though you cannot allege a single reason why you should take it. Yet take it "without a cause."'

'No one who is anxious to have a Saviour has committed the unpardonable sin.'

'What God does in saving Gospel-hearers is to show them *with* power what they have previously known *without* power.'

'Our unwillingness is our inability.'

'"There is no man that sinneth not;" this truth is the hypocrite's pillow, but the believer's bed of thorns.'

'Christ is the lever by which God moves a world of souls.'

'God does not say, "Pay what you *can*," but "Pay what you *owe*."'

'A cloak of profession will make an awful blaze in that day when He burns the stubble.'

'God is a sin-hater, but a soul-lover.'

'The natural heart keeps no record of sin; it is only God's law which does so.'

'The Shepherd can number His sheep, but the sheep can't. Christ's favourite expression, when speaking of His saved ones, is "many." Our Shorter Catechism

should have said, "elected *many* to everlasting life."
I am not sure but we shall be in the majority yet when
we are gathered into the kingdom.'

'The Ransom-money is the only current coin at the
court of heaven, and it has the resurrection stamp upon
it. We used to speak of a "king's ransom," but guess,
if you can, what the value must be of a ransom that
sets free nations, kingdoms, peoples!'

'Lord, we bespeak blessing for to-morrow' was often
his prayer on Saturday evening at family worship; and
he went into the pulpit in the expectation that this
prayer would be answered. Many of the worshippers
were brought, by his opening prayer in church, into
the very presence of God, and felt that they needed no
more to strengthen them for that day's journey through
the wilderness. Some of his petitions are graven on the
memory of his hearers :—

'Good Shepherd, gratify Thyself by saving me!'

'Remember us, O Lord! and when we have said this we
have said everything, for Thou knowest what to do next.'

'Thou dost not give away the children's bread.
Surely, then, thou keepest it for the children. Give it
now to us.'

'Give us a taste of the grapes of Eshcol that we may
long for the Promised Land.'

'Lord, before we put in the sickle, we ask Thee to
whet it.'

'When we pray in the morning to be filled with the
Spirit, may we expect to be filled all day with thoughts
of Christ.'

'Let us be as watchful after the victory as before the
battle.'

'When we are forgetting Thee, recall us to communion with Thyself by some text, some word of Thine
own.'

'O make us sincere to the core of our heart by the help of Thy Holy Spirit, for it's not natural!'

'Awake, awake, put on strength, O arm of the Lord! that arm that has plucked many a brand from the burning, and has been folded round many a lamb!'

'"Visit us with Thy salvation"—for there are folds and folds of the robe of righteousness that we would fain have Thee to unfold to us.'

'We ask for conviction. We do not ask that it may be very deep, for we make idols of so many things that we might make an idol of our conviction. So we do not say anything about the depth, but we ask for the reality.'

'If our hands that should grasp the heavenly treasure are kept closed because they are filled with earthly things, *deal with us*, Lord, until we stretch out empty hands, suppliants for Thy blessing.'

'If Thy people cannot say they have come to the land where "they hunger no more, neither thirst any more," they can at least say they neither hunger nor thirst while the Lamb is leading them through the desert.'

'Let us seek to be delivered from trifling prayers and contentment with trifling answers,' he once said solemnly; and at another time, 'Is not this a lamentable state of things that there should be so much to get and so few to ask!' Closet prayer he considered as 'an ordinance of God for every believer,' affecting all the providences of a day, and closely linked with meditation on the Word. 'You say, "If I pray I'll prosper." That is only half the truth. If you meditate on the Word and pray, you'll prosper.' 'Prayer will be very lame and dry if it does not come from reading the Scriptures.' 'May we be able to spread our Bibles on the Mercy-seat, and read them by the light of the cloud of glory,' he once prayed. He spoke of prayer as 'seed sown on the heart of God;' meditation, as 'letting God speak to us till our heart is throbbing;' and fasting, as 'abstaining from all that interferes with prayer.'

'I do not think,' he said, 'we ever pray the Lord's Prayer with all our heart, without laying up something we shall be thankful for in the future.'

'It is not right for God's people to say when a matter for prayer is put before them, "O, what can *my* prayers do?" What can *your God do*?'

'God likes to see His people shut up to this, that there is no hope but in prayer. Herein lies the Church's power against the world.'

'It is a sign the blessing is not at hand when God's people are not praying much.'

'Hezekiah's prayer got a large answer. When you send in a petition to the Lord leave a wide margin that He may write a great deal on it.'

'Always follow your work with believing prayer' was his counsel to a busy worker. When presiding at a district prayer-meeting, a request for prayer was handed in by a woman whose 'husband had gone amissing.' Dr. Bonar began his prayer thus: 'O Lord, here is a sad case,—a man amissing. Thou wast once amissing Thyself, but Thy parents sought Thee till they found Thee in the Temple. Lord, seek and find this poor man and restore him to his wife and family.' At the close of a missionary meeting he was asked to pray, and in doing so drew the thoughts of those present to the Lord's promise to His Son in the Second Psalm: 'Ask of Me, and I shall give Thee the heathen for thine inheritance,' etc. His solemn closing appeal sent a thrill through the audience: 'Saviour, *ask, and the Father will give Thee.*' After illustrating the truth that God gives us as much as we ask for by the story of Joseph's brethren getting all the

sacks filled that they brought to him, he said in prayer :
'O Lord, Thou art our Joseph. We bring to Thee our
empty sacks. Do Thou fill them all ! '

One Sabbath, when explaining to the children how
when they were weak then they were strong, he referred
to the fact that the finest fruits, such as grapes and
melons, grow upon stalks so weak that if left to themselves they would trail along the ground, never ripen, and
be destroyed. The gardener has to prop them up and
support them firmly that they may grow and come to
perfection. In like manner the Good Gardener has to
tend and support His weak plants, and to graft them
into the True Vine, that they may grow in Him and
bring forth fruit fit for the Master's use. Then he
offered the touching request : 'Lord, pity the weakness
of the plants that bear the fruit of the Spirit.'

His prayer one New Year's Day was memorable to
those who were present :—

'Thou tellest our wanderings, and Thou hast been
writing an account of our lives up till this date. This
year Thou hast begun a new chapter. Lord, may there
be always in it something about Thy glory. " This day
My servant gave a cup of cold water and plucked a
brand from the burning." Perhaps Thou wilt come
Thyself this year, and finish the record by telling that
at this point Thou didst come Thyself with the crown ! '

His thanksgiving-prayers on Communion Sabbaths
will long be remembered, and many of his requests before
and at the Tables.

'The clouds which have arisen from the marshes of
our sins need new bursts of the Sun of righteousness to
melt them away. Shine forth ! shine forth ! '

'As the bread is broken and the wine is poured out,
may we feel that He is scarcely an absent Saviour,
though unseen.'

'As we get into the enjoyment of Thy love may we find that we need scarcely any other heaven either here or hereafter—only more of that love and the continuance of it.'

'Lord, if Thou lookest for us, Thou wilt find us under the apple-tree.'

At the close of the Communion Sabbath in October, 1886, Mr. Inglis of Dundee, who had been assisting in the services, asked prayer for himself and his people. Dr. Bonar took up the request in his closing prayer :—

'Lord Jesus, Thou art the Intercessor. Present his petition to the Father, and add our names to it, for blessing on himself and his elders, on his congregation, on his missionary. And one thing more, Lord Jesus, come quickly Thyself!'

The old-fashioned form of service was always retained in Finnieston : the Action Sermon, the Fencing [1] of the Table, the three Tables following, and then the Closing Address with its message to old and young. The fragrance of these services and the words then spoken, still linger in the hearts of many of God's children.

'At the Table, remember Christ and forget yourself.'

'Jesus is walking to-day among the seven golden candlesticks, and He will stop here, at our Communion Table, to see if any of you want anything from Him.'

'There is nothing between a sinner and the Saviour, but there *is* something between the sinner and the Lord's Table.'

'However weak you are, if you value supremely the atoning blood, come to the Table.'

---

[1] 'Fencing,' he always explained as declaring by whose authority the Table was spread. The word is used in old Scotch law.

'God's people have a ravenous hunger for a crucified Christ.'

'"Little children" is the name for the family of God in every place and at every time. John learned the name from Christ at the first Communion Table. He only said it once, and John, leaning on His bosom, caught it up and repeated it.'

'At the Lord's Supper (John xiii. to xvi.) the characteristics of six of the disciples are seen. John, the type of a true communicant, realising his own sinfulness and liability to fall, but yet not rising from his place on Christ's bosom. Judas, to outward appearance as near as John, but an unworthy communicant, hardened, often warned, but to no purpose. Peter, ardent and warm-hearted, but one who yielded too much to feeling, forgetting that feelings fail, though faith does not. Thomas, a suspicious, questioning, sad cast of mind, but a real disciple. Jude, a thoughtful, growing Christian. Philip, a slow mind, from want of meditation and reflection, not grasping the truth sufficiently.'

Many years ago, a lady from a neighbouring congregation took shelter from the rain in the porch of Finnieston Church, on a Communion Sabbath, while Dr. Bonar was giving an address from Matt. xxvi. 48: 'That same is He: *hold Him fast.*' She could not hear the address, but over and over again, as she stood in the porch, the words of the text came to her ear like a message from the Lord, 'That same is He: *hold Him fast.*' The first part of the closing address was specially for the children, who always gathered in the front seats of the gallery, and were quiet and interested spectators while the bread and wine were handed to the communicants. Sometimes their thoughts were directed to a Communion time of long ago on the heathery moors, under the open sky, or to Communion Sabbaths

not so long before, in the days of the minister's own
boyhood, in Lady Glenorchy's Chapel in Edinburgh.
When pressing the children to come to Christ, and then,
with their parents, to come to the Lord's Table, he told
the story of an old gentleman whom he remembered in
the Chapel, who did not become a communicant till he
was fifty years of age.   He did not know the Lord when
he first went to speak to the minister, Dr. Jones, about
joining the church, and he told him he was not ready to
become a communicant.   It was not till he had come
back six times that he was able to say he knew the
Lord, and had a right to come to His Table.   In apply-
ing the story to the children Dr. Bonar told them he
wanted them to be like that good old man, 'not in
being so long of coming, but in being sure that you are
saved before you come.   It is the same bread for the
grown people and for the children.   I am an older man
now than almost any of my congregation, and I find I
give out the same food I need for myself.'

The address never concluded without reference to the
Lord's Second Coming as the motive for more earnest
work, and more earnest prayer.

'Do much, and say little about it, and think not
about what brethren say of you.   Pray much, and you
will be very near the King, for He has a special love to
petitions.'

' "Behold, I come quickly."   O sinner, are you ready
for that long eternity?   What if it comes to you some
day suddenly?   O believer, have you done all you
would fain do?   Is it no fault of yours if souls are not
saved?   O elders, are you devising means for winning
souls?   O deacons, are you like Stephen, of whom
I often say he thought in the midst of his deacon's
work how to commend his Lord?   O people of God,
are you remembering that "*quickly*"?   Time is short.

Are you praying much? Are you letting your light shine?'

'Christ's nearer coming casts deeper solemnity over every Communion.'

The day's services were always brought to a close by singing three verses of the Ninety-eighth Psalm:—

> 'With harp, with harp, and voice of psalms,
>   Unto JEHOVAH sing:
> With trumpets, cornets, gladly sound
>   Before the Lord the King.
>
> Let seas and all their fulness roar;
>   The world, and dwellers there;
> Let floods clap hands, and let the hills
>   Together joy declare
>
> Before the Lord; because He comes,
>   To judge the earth comes He;
> He'll judge the world with righteousness,
>   His folk with equity.'

This custom, begun in Collace, was continued in Finnieston, and wherever or whenever that psalm is sung it will always stir the heart of Dr. Bonar's old hearers, bringing back hallowed recollections of 'days of heaven upon earth.'

A BASKET OF FRAGMENTS

'I beseech you to keep Christ, for I did what I could to put you within grips of Him. I told you Christ's testament and latter-will plainly, and I kept nothing back that my Lord gave me. I gave Christ to you with good-will.'—*Samuel Rutherford.*

CHAPTER V

THERE was no part of a minister's work which he did not try to render useful both to himself and to others. A marriage, a baptism, a funeral, were all opportunities for good. At Collace, he heard of a woman awakened by his address at her marriage ceremony.[1] He sometimes, on such occasions, referred to Proverbs xii. 4 : ' A virtuous woman is a crown to her husband,' and paraphrased it thus : ' She makes his house a palace, and himself a king.' 'Remember,' he would say, 'God grudges you nothing if you take it from His hands through Christ.' At other times, he spoke of husband and wife as 'helpmeets,' and compared them to the two sides of an arch, with love as the keystone : ' And see what burdens an arch can bear ! '

The baptismal service was never a mere form, but a time when all the congregation felt that Father, Son, and Holy Ghost were drawing near to bless.

' The sacraments of the New Testament are signs between Heaven and earth. Baptism is a sign from Heaven that God remembers little children, and looks upon them in love, saying, "Suffer little children to come unto Me," etc. The Lord's Supper is a sign from earth to Heaven that we remember our Lord's dying command : ' This do in remembrance of Me " ; and keep it till He come.'

[1] See *Diary and Letters*, p. 119.

' I consider the baptism of infants to be, not a confession of our faith, but of God's interest in us. I am in the way of putting it thus : "Remember, parents, to tell your children that on the day of baptism they were presented to the Three Persons, and the water was meant to be a sign and seal that Father, Son, and Holy Spirit offered salvation to them. Ask them, have you accepted the gift offered ? '

He called on a young mother in Collace soon after the birth of her first-born son, and, after asking what name she meant to give the baby, he said, ' I never knew the meaning of these words in Psalm ciii.— ' Like as a father pitieth his children,' etc.—till I heard my own little infant cry. How I pitied her, how I wanted to help her, and yet I couldn't ! ' When the parents brought the child to be baptized a few weeks afterwards, he gave him the name ' William,' though he had not been reminded of it. After the service he said to them, ' Ah, you forgot to write down the baby's name, but there will be no mistake about it on that day when it is written in the Lamb's Book of Life.'

' How solemn it is for you,' he said to another before the baptism of her little one, ' to look on that child and wonder, " will that head ever wear a crown of glory ? and will these lips ever sing His praises ? and will these eyes ever see the King in His beauty ? " '

One Friday evening a stranger from the Highlands came to the manse to ask that his baby might be baptized on the following Sabbath. While talking with him Dr. Bonar found that he was not a communicant, though evidently a converted man. He asked him why he was not, and the man replied that a very peculiar experience was needed to fit any one for going to the Lord's Table. Dr. Bonar tried to show him that an interest in Christ was sufficient, but the man still kept

to his point. At last, seeing he was deeply in earnest,
he told him he could not baptize his child on the coming
Sabbath, but asked him to go home and search the New
Testament for the qualifications laid down as necessary
for admission to the Lord's Table, and to return in a
fortnight and tell him what he had found. The man
came back at the time appointed, but with a very
different expression on his face. He and his wife had
looked through the New Testament, but could find no
extraordinary experience mentioned as necessary, so he
was ready now to go to the Lord's Table. His after-
life testified to his sincerity and faith in Christ.

At a baptism on one occasion, he spoke to the
parents about Jesus as being the only holy child ever
born on our earth. The mother reminded him of this
when her baby was taken away soon after, and added,
' My little one is just as spotless now.'

His love for the children showed itself in the interest
with which he followed them year by year. Each had
a place in his prayers, and they fully returned his affection. They would linger in the church as he went from
the pulpit to the vestry, in the hope of having his hand
laid on their head, and hearing him call them by their
name. One little child called him 'the minister with
the laughing face.' It was not uncommon in Collace to
see groups of children round him as he rode about from
place to place on his pony. One of the touching sights
on the day on which he was buried, was that of the
children round the grave, with their sad and wistful
faces. Some time after his death, a little child was
heard praying, 'O God, bless Mr. M'Intyre, and send
back Dr. Bonar, for we're wearying to see him!' He
spoke with unhesitating certainty of the conversion of
children.

' We ask Thee, Lord, to raise up a generation of

believing children. We do not ask Thee for a generation of believers, but of believing children. " Is anything too hard for the Lord ? " Faith is a gift, and a gift that a child can take.'

'A young hand may be placed on the head of the scapegoat as well as an old hand.'

'God's heart is so quick and so tender that He can hear the hosanna of a little child.'

' " Out of the mouth of babes and sucklings Thou hast perfected praise "—Thou hast filled up the choir of heaven.'

'Christ would have wanted one of the marks of Incarnate God if the story of His blessing the little children had not been narrated, for "Behold, God is mighty and despiseth not any." '

The Apostle Matthew, he used to say, must have been very fond of children, for his Gospel is full of references to them. He thought Paul must have been a famous preacher to children, for he had so much to tell about. He had been in perils of waters, in perils of robbers, in perils in the sea, in shipwrecks, etc. And he did preach to the children, for he witnessed 'both to small and great' (Acts xxvi. 22).

Wherever he went, he liked to visit the Sabbath school, and used to urge other ministers to provide something specially for the children on Communion Sabbaths. At Crossford, where he often visited his friend Mr. Manson, he was not unfrequently the means of helping and cheering the teachers in their work. His words are still remembered : 'Be sure and aim at the conversion of the children. They are never too young to come to Jesus. I hope you pray for each of your scholars by name. That has a wonderful effect on your teaching. Never come to your classes without first being in prayer.' 'Kindness to those you teach is part of the teaching,' he used to say. In a country village where he was staying, he was told that the children had a bad habit of running after passing carriages. He took the opportunity at a children's meeting in the evening of asking them to tell him the name of the only man we read of in the Bible who ran after a carriage. The answer was 'Gehazi; and he was not a man to be imitated!'

Not being able to be present one evening at the monthly meeting of his Sabbath-school teachers, he sent the following *Report* to the Superintendent:—

'MEETING OF TEACHERS IN JERUSALEM

(2 Chron. xxx. 22)

MONTH OF ABIB, A.C. 726

'*The Superintendent.*—The King; his name Hezekiah, *i.e.* "Jehovah is my strength."

'*The Teachers.*—Levites who "taught the good knowledge of the Lord. Some of them discouraged; they spoke of their difficulties, those they taught not always caring for their teaching, and many of them very dull in understanding. Some of the teachers spoke of fancying they had not the gift of teaching, and should resign.

'*The Superintendent's Address.*—Hezekiah "spake to the heart" (see margin). Hezekiah "spake to . . . all." Hezekiah reminded them that their theme was "the knowledge of the Lord." It was a royal and hearty word in season. *N.B.*—A note of his address: "My friend Isaiah reminds me that it is this knowledge that is to fill the earth one day, as the waters cover the sea. Go on, then. Tell the "Good Tidings." Tell them to reason with our God, who can make their scarlet sins disappear, and their souls be whiter than the snow, through the "good knowledge" of Him who is to come.

'The meeting was held in the hall on Mount Zion, within sight of the palace. It was a very happy meeting. Our reporter refers to the lively "singing and the great gladness;" and mention is made of the prayers also going up to Jehovah's dwelling-place.'

His interest in the members of his young women's Bible-class was unwearied, and many owe their first religious impressions to his faithful lessons. To them, as to the members of the young men's class, he succeeded in imparting a love for God's Word and for Scripture truth which became characteristic of them.

One Tuesday evening at the class, he referred to 'the bricks of Babylon'—how every brick had on it the king's stamp. 'So,' he said, 'everything we do should have the King's stamp on it.' One of his hearers, not long after, was set to the tedious work of cleaning a feather-bed. Many a time she felt tempted to hurry over it, but 'the bricks of Babylon' kept ringing in her ears, and she had to do it all faithfully. When Dr. Bonar called to see her, she said to him, 'O these bricks of Babylon were a trouble to me!' 'Were they on your dusters and brooms?' he asked. 'No, on a feather-bed!' she replied, to his great amusement. The story was repeated to a servant, who said, 'Well, I hate cleaning the knives, but I can't but do them thoroughly now.'

Nowhere, perhaps, was his personal influence more strongly felt than in his young men's Bible-class, and there was no part of his work which in his later years he gave up more reluctantly. Its first place of meeting was in the little room behind the old church, where for many a year, in spite of discomfort and inconvenience, the young men gathered round the teacher, who was ever bringing to them out of his treasure things new and old. One book of Scripture after another was opened up with unfailing freshness and originality. Not long before his death he was singularly pleased with a letter he received from one who for years had wandered about the world, and had carried with him, through all his vicissitudes, the memory of Sabbath evenings in the Bible-class. 'After seeing so much of

the world, and, after passing my fortieth year, there is
nothing which has so deeply impressed itself on my life,
and engrained itself into my very existence, as the
solemn lessons you taught us in your Bible-class.' And
when pressed by temptation and the allurements of sin
on every side, 'there were silent voices speaking to me
from that Bible-class which I dared not disobey.'

When members of the class left town or went abroad,
he was never too busy to write to them, and their letters
were a source of constant interest and pleasure to him.
The young men, on their part, felt the sympathy of a
heart that was always young. In his busiest time he
has been known to call on a young man in his lodgings
at ten o'clock at night, hoping to find him at home then,
as he had been unsuccessful before. He would go far
out of his way on a Sabbath evening to take a young
man with him to the class, walking along with his arm
in his, and chatting in a way that put him entirely at
his ease. A question as to his spiritual welfare would
be accompanied by a kindly touch of his hand on the
young man's shoulder. 'That touch remains with me
still,' said one, long years after.

Sometimes he had a gathering of the students connected with the church at his house, and these meetings
he always greatly enjoyed.

'Last night,' he writes of one such occasion, 'I had at
my house a gathering of students connected with the
congregation—about thirty. . . . At worship I showed
them that Paul went to college at Jerusalem,—was a
clever student,—had for his professor Gamaliel, the very
best in his line,—imbibed all his views, etc. But the
Lord transferred him to another college, when he, at a
holiday time, had taken a trip to Damascus, and had
offered to be of any use to his idol, Gamaliel.'

At the close of one of these gatherings he prayed

with peculiar solemnity : ' And when we all meet together again, may it be with our bosom filled with sheaves ! '

The young men who used to gather together in Finnieston, are scattered now all over the world. The meeting-time has not yet come, but when it does, it will be true of them : ' these shall come from far ; and, lo, these from the north and from the west ; and these from the land of Sinim.'

AMONG HIS PEOPLE

'I think I have got more good from visiting my people than from any book of practical theology I ever read.'—*A. A. B.*

CHAPTER VI

To the members of his congregation Dr. Bonar was both friend and father. Not only was he quick to recognise their faces, but their different circumstances touched and interested him, and made him feel his visitation a pleasure and benefit to himself as well as to them. ' He was that ta'en up aboot *me*,' were the words of one of them, as she recalled his thoughtful interest in her in times of need.

How much importance he attached to this part of a pastor's work is shown in a letter written to Dr. Somerville from Collace in the year 1850 :—

'. . . There is a blessing resting on visiting. What else is fitted to make us know the state of our flocks? Were it not for their good but only for our own, is not this department of work most important? It is only thus we can know our people's spiritual state, and I would go on in this work weekly, if not daily, even if not a soul got good from it but myself. I see the sad wounds of my flock—I see their slow growth in grace—I discover how few really are awakened, how few are in earnest, how very few are saved. It is humbling and painful beyond most things. Of course, there is a kind of visiting which is simply useless, if not hurtful, to minister and people, but visiting with this design is truly soul-exercise. It is a luxury oftentimes to find out truth in the Word, and prepare our sermons for the people, so we need this self-denying mixture to temper our preparations. I daresay you admit all this as much as I do, and yet still cry, " O for a way of profitably visiting !" Dear brother, this is the gift of God. Holiness of heart and life is what I find I need more than anything, a heart daily filled and burning with fresh views of divine love. This is what I seldom have in visiting, and yet I see that if I had that, it would make visiting like the gardener going among his plants and watering them as he saw need, while the Sabbath sermons would be the heavy showers.'

His methods of finding out the state of his people's minds were often very ingenious. He and some other ministers were discussing this subject one day. He said, 'I find it a very good plan to ask when I am visiting, "What was your chapter at family worship this morning?" In this way I find out whether they *have* family worship, and if they have paid attention to it!'

He used to tell with great enjoyment of a remark made by some women as they watched him passing their door in the mission district. 'Why does Dr. Bonar walk so fast?' said one of them. 'Why,' said another, 'do you not know the messengers of the gospel must go swiftly?'

One day he called on a good woman, and found her busy at her washing-tub. 'O Doctor,' was her salutation, 'you always find me in a mess.' 'But there's some one helping you,' he replied. 'No,' she said wonderingly. 'Yes,' he said, 'your Elder Brother is with you.' 'From that day to this,' said the good woman, 'I have never begun a day's work without remembering "My Elder Brother is with me."'

One who was attending his communicants' class told him that she was not yet one of God's children, but was very anxious about her soul. She had been brought up carefully, but had been taught more of the Law than of the Gospel, and it was hard for her to believe that salvation could be hers by the simple acceptance of Christ. While talking with her one day, Dr. Bonar drew a hymn-book out of his pocket and read the well-known lines :—

> 'Nothing either great or small—
> Nothing, sinner, no ;
> Jesus did it, did it all,
> Long, long ago.'

Then he said to her, 'I think you are trying to put a bit to Christ's robe of righteousness.' The words rang in her ears all day, and, just before going to bed, the light shone into her heart, and she saw the simplicity of the way of salvation. She said, 'I felt full of shame to think I had been doing such a thing.' From day to day she went on feeding on the truth, and learning more and more of the Word of God from her pastor's lips ; but she had not openly confessed Christ to those around her, though she felt she ought to do so. 'One evening at the prayer-meeting,' she said, 'I got the word I had been waiting for for six months. Dr. Bonar was speaking about the "anointing oil," in Exodus xxx. 22-32, as a type of the Holy Spirit given to believers. "Some of you," he said, "have had the oil poured over you, but *you wipe off the drops with your hand.*"'

When calling on a member of his congregation one day, she said to him, 'Do you know how I first came to know I was saved ? I dreamed that you were talking to me, and at last, as you rose to go away, you said, "So you don't want to be indebted to Another?" I awoke and saw it all.'

To an aged member of his flock he said, 'You must keep fast hold of the text which was written for you : "Even to your old age I am He ; and even to hoar hairs will I carry you " (Isaiah xlvi. 4). Just as you carried the children when they were young, so the Lord says He will carry you now when you are old.' His words dropped by the wayside were the seeds of life to many. A Sabbath scholar never forgot the impression made upon him by the minister putting his hand on his shoulder one night and saying, 'Matthew, be like Matthew the publican. He left all, rose up, and followed Jesus.' Meeting a young friend on the street he asked her what her name was. She said, 'Christina.' 'Well,' he said, 'you have Christ in your name. I hope you have Him in your heart.' One November afternoon he called upon a student who had just joined his Bible-class. The sun was shining into the room, and Dr. Bonar remarked upon it and said, 'I am sure it does not hinder you in your studies; and if you have the Sun of righteousness shining in your heart would it not help you?' When visiting one who was ill, he turned to a stranger who was sitting in the room, and asked her if her name was in the Lamb's Book of Life? She said, 'Oh, sir, my name is not in your books.' 'Oh no,' he said, 'not in my books, but is it in the Lamb's Book?' 'I hope so,' she replied, and quoted the verse, 'If we hope for that we see not,' etc. 'Oh, but that is not the meaning of the verse at all,' said Dr. Bonar, 'you must have more than a hope,' and he showed how she might even now know that her name was in the Book of Life. The conversation was blessed to her, and she became a true child of God.

His acts of loving ministry were countless. He would toil up long flights of stairs to take a new remedy to some one in pain, or to find lodgings for one who was friendless and homeless. He would carry a bottle of beef tea in his pocket to a sickly woman, or a picture-book to while away the long hours of a child's illness. A servant who had belonged to the church left for a situation in the south of England, where she remained for fifteen years. During all that time, Dr. Bonar wrote frequently to her, and sent her each of his little books as they were published, 'and,' she said, 'I am only one of many to whom he did the same.' No service was too small for him to do for any of Christ's little ones, and the joy of his service was as remarkable as its ceaseless-ness. 'Love is the *motive* for working,' he used to say, 'joy is the *strength* for working.' His sunny face as he came into a sick-room brought healing with it, and his brightness was infectious. ' Now, remember,' he said to some friends in parting, ' whenever I see you looking sad or downcast, I will ask you when you cut the Book of Psalms out of the Bible ! '

One day he called on an invalid and said, ' I have brought you a new medicine.' ' What is it ? ' she asked, ' Here it is. " A merry heart doeth good like a medicine ! " '

If sent for to pray with careless people when dying he seldom or never refused, but he did not consider it a necessity to go. He thought they made it a sort of extreme unction ; but to visit God's people in sickness he considered a duty. Ministering to the ' household of faith ' was a form of service he constantly pressed upon others, and presented to them in various aspects. ' It is no small matter to help one another,' he would say. ' To keep a believer's lamp bright is one of the highest benefits you can confer on a dark world.' ' God loves His saints so much that He will give a reward to any one who gives one of them a cup of cold water ! '

' Paul says that, even for the sake of comforting the saints, he would wish to abide in the flesh.'

After preaching in Dudhope Church, Dundee, one Sabbath, upon John the Baptist in prison, a gentleman came into the vestry and said to him, ' I am going to see a dying elder, I will try to tell him what you have been saying.' ' Ay,' said Dr. Bonar, ' and tell him Christ will come to visit *him*, though He did not go to visit John ; that was for our sake.' His friend, Mr. Manson, when laid aside by illness, had spoken of himself as a ' cumberer of the ground.' Dr. Bonar wrote to him :—

' You say it is not wonderful that you are not getting strength, for you are " only a cumberer." Brother, it is cumberers that are spared ! '

His sympathy with those in sorrow had been learned by passing through the same sad discipline. When Mrs. Bonar was so unexpectedly taken away from him in October, 1864, he wrote to his brother Horatius:—

'I think that the Lord who used to give me health to work is now saying, "Will you seek to glorify Me by bearing and enduring?"'

To other friends he wrote:—

'Our time is shortening. The Master has been reminding me of this very solemnly, changing the blue sky over my head by the shade of lasting sorrow.

"But yet I know I shall Him praise."'

'We must learn more and more how to *suffer*. "Thy will be done" is one of the heavenly plants that Jesus left the seed of when He was here. We must cultivate it in our garden. And so also there is another, "The Lord thinketh upon me,"—a plant cultivated by King David when he was an exile in the wilds of En-gedi. This plant is the believer's "Forget-me-not."'

An old friend had been talking with him one day, soon after Mrs. Bonar's death, and as they referred to the many friends who had gone before, and specially to his own great loss, Dr. Bonar was for a few moments quite overcome. Then, quickly recovering himself, he said in his bright way, 'But the best is yet to come!' He had been engaged to give an address to the Young Men's Literary Society on an evening just a day or two after Mrs. Bonar's funeral. He could not take the subject he had intended, but he came as he had promised, and gave an address on some things connected with the Holy Land. The inexpressible sadness of his whole appearance, and his marvellous self-control, made a deep impression on all who were present. 'God does not tell us,' he said, 'to *feel* it is for the best, but he does ask us to *believe* it.'

'Master, that disciple is weeping,' would be enough to

draw the Saviour's attention when on earth. And we can all so speak to Him still.'

'I often read at funerals the twenty-first chapter of Revelation, and I do it with this connection in my mind: "There shall be no more sorrow, nor death, nor pain, nor crying," and "I will give of the fountain of the water of life freely." I always feel that the Lord wanted to put these things within sight of one another. If we would draw more of the living water from the wells of salvation, we should have less sorrow. Drink more, believer. What aileth thee, Hagar? The well is just beside thee. Drink, and go on your way.'

Hearing of the sudden death of one of his people he hastened to the house to see the daughter who was left an orphan. He did not say almost anything to her, but gently put his arm round her and laid her head on his shoulder. When the news of his own sudden removal passed from one to another, from many lips broke the sorrowful words, 'I have lost my best earthly friend!' and some wept for him as they had never wept for any friend on earth before.

It was often a matter of surprise that strong and vigorous as he was himself, he could sympathise so tenderly with the sick and suffering. His words to them were always full of comfort.

'It is worth while being wounded to have the hands of the Great Physician upon you.'

'If we cannot say like Paul "this light affliction," let us at any rate try to say, "It is but for a moment."'

'Those who sing loudest in the kingdom will be those who on earth had the greatest bodily suffering. We pity them now, but then we shall almost envy them.'

'We have got more from Paul's prison-house than from his visit to the third heavens.'

'A believer is an Æolian harp, and every event of his life is just the passing wind drawing out the music. And God hears it.'

'"In the world ye shall have tribulation," *but draw the closer to Me.*'

There were two thoughts he often left with God's people in sickness. One was that they might do a great work for the Lord by praying much, and that it is really promotion to be, not down in the valley with Joshua, but with Aaron and Hur on the mountain-top. The other thought was that they are *teaching angels* (Eph. iii. 10). Angels learn much by visiting God's people. They know nothing of suffering themselves, but they learn from the patience and joyfulness of suffering believers. When the sick one enters heaven, some of the angels will say, 'Oh, here is my teacher come!'

Many outside of his own congregation sent for him in times of sickness or trouble. One Saturday evening a lady called at the manse and begged him to go to see her son, who was hopelessly ill. As he went into the room the young man closed a ledger that was lying on the table before him, and said, 'There, now, I've written the last word I'll ever write in it.' 'And what then?' asked Dr. Bonar. They drew their chairs to the fireside and began to talk together. Little by little the Spirit of God began to work, and the dying man was led to Christ. His joy was quite unusual—so great that his mother was afraid it might be a delusion. One day when Dr. Bonar was with him, he said to him, 'You will be experiencing something of the joy unspeakable.' 'It's more than that,' said the dying man, 'it is so great. It is joy *unthinkable.*' A young man, whom he visited at another time, was brought to the Saviour on his deathbed, and filled with great peace in believing. He had been careless and worldly until he was taken ill. One day listening to a brass band playing under his window, the tune recalled to him former scenes of gaiety in which he had taken part, and the thought, 'Am I going into eternity with all these sins upon my soul?' forced itself upon him, and was the means of his awakening. As he drew near his end, he one day said to Dr. Bonar, 'Do you think my mind can be growing weak, for I don't care now for any but the common texts, such as "The Son of man is come to seek and to save that which is lost!"' Shortly before his death he said, 'Jesus came so near to me last night, that I almost felt Him breathing.'

Not long before his death Dr. Bonar was asked to visit a family in great affliction. They were not members of his church, but he went at once, and continued his visits till they were no longer needed. Both father and daughter were dying at the same time. The former was full of joy at the prospect of being with Jesus, and could sing of victory in the midst of great bodily weakness. With the daughter it was different. She had peace, but not the confident assurance and joy that her father had. This troubled her not a little, and she told Dr. Bonar how it distressed her. He said, 'Well, Jeanie, you have peace, have you not? You are resting on what the Lord Jesus has done for you? You see your father was much older when he came to the Lord, and he had more to be forgiven. Consequently his joy at so many sins forgiven is greater than yours.' This answer cheered and comforted her, and so much blessing did she get from his continued visits that she longed daily and hourly for them. Six weeks after her father's death she fell asleep in Jesus on a Sabbath morning. Throughout the day before, whenever there was a ring or knock at the door, she said to her mother, 'I hope this is Dr. Bonar now, mother!' Shortly before she passed away she was heard saying, 'Do come now, quickly, Lord Jesus. Oh, please do come!'

A young woman was taken to the hospital, incurably ill. Dr. Bonar went to see her, and before leaving said to her, 'Remember us in prayer.' She had been feeling very sad, and these words were like new life to her. It was not 'we will remember you,' but 'you will remember us'; and she saw there was still work for her to do, though laid on a bed of sickness.

One who suffered much said when he asked her if she were not longing to be at rest, 'No, I am not wearying for death, but I do hope the Lord may come before I die!'

'Think upon the Lord when you can, and He will think upon you when you can't,' he used to say to sick people. In all his visitation, fear in going to cases of sickness was unknown to him. During the smallpox epidemic in Glasgow he visited some patients week after week. When missionary in St. George's, Edinburgh, he visited a man so ill with typhus fever that no one else would go near him. His kindness touched the sick man's heart, and made him willing to receive the truth. This fearlessness characterised him in every point of duty. He was a firm and determined total abstainer, long before total abstinence was much spoken of, and was not afraid to denounce the drinking customs of the country wherever he went, as well as from his own pulpit. When he first went to Collace he gave great offence by refusing to drink the whisky which was always offered to him when visiting, and the young minister was pronounced to be 'awfu' proud.' However, when it was understood that he would take milk or cream instead, it became an invariable custom to give it to him. One old woman, as she gave him a glass of milk, said, 'It's rale nice, sir, it's the sap o' Macbeth's Castle!' Before he had been long in Collace the one public-house in the parish was closed through his efforts, along with Mr Nairne's influence; and it has never been reopened. In Finnieston district more than one poor drunkard was brought out of bondage into the liberty of Christ through his personal instrumentality. An earnest and consistent member of the church dates the beginning of his changed life to one Saturday evening, when Dr. Bonar found him near the door of the Mission-hall, and, drawing his arm within his own, led him upstairs into the Gospel Temperance Meeting. That night the man signed the pledge, and became soon after a believer in the Lord Jesus Christ.

At a meeting of the 'Mizpah Band' in Glasgow, formed chiefly of those who had been reclaimed from drunkenness, Mr. Moody turned to him after several had given their testimony and said, 'Now, Dr. Bonar, give us *your* testimony.' He at once rose and said, 'Mr. Moody, I have no testimony to give, for I was free-born!'

When giving reproof, he was as faithful and fearless in carrying out the Apostle's injunction: 'reprove, rebuke, exhort,' but in a way that seldom gave offence. He used to say, 'A man is never safe in rebuking another if it does not cost him something to have to do it.'

'Look at Christ's gentleness in His dealings with us. We never find a ruffle of irritation on His lips. When He wants to reprove the forwardness of His disciples, He does it by a little child. Was there ever a gentler reproof given to a backslider than that given to Peter: "Simon, son of Jonas, *lovest thou Me?*"'

'It is a test of our progress in sanctification if we are

willing to have our faults pointed out to us, without getting angry. Why should we take offence at being told we are not perfect?'

'God tells us to love reproof. I don't know any one who ever took rebuke better than Eli. "It is the Lord!" When Nathan said to David, "Thou art the man," he did not flare up as Herod did. No. He said "I have sinned," and went away to write the Fifty-first Psalm.'

An old lady in his congregation used always to sit in one particular part of her room, because when she lifted her eyes from her work she could see Dr. Bonar's portrait on the wall. 'His eyes always rebuke me,' she said, 'whether in his picture or in himself. These other ministers whom I used to be with, they just agreed with me in everything I said, but catch Dr. Bonar doing that!'

He was asked to visit an invalid lady whom he did not know, and found her suffering from nervous depression. After he had talked with her he said before leaving, 'Now, you have far too little to do. I am going to give you something to find out for me,' and left her some Bible exercises to work out. She grew quite interested in her new employment, and in a short time was nearly well. A mother told him how for twenty-four years she had prayed and made efforts for her son's conversion, but he was still unsaved. Dr. Bonar said, 'Speak less *to* him and speak more to God *about* him.' The remark repeated to the young man impressed him much, and not long after he was brought to Christ.

He was told of a woman in the mission district who professed to have been converted. After he had been to see her, he said he did not think she was really changed, or her house would have been cleaner. He was quite right, for the woman's profession turned out to be insincere.

A gentleman whom he knew to be very excitable told him that during his illness he had had a vision of angels, and had felt one of them touch him as he lay in bed. Dr. Bonar quietly remarked, ' Have you a cat in the house? Don't you think it may have been the cat ?'

Sometimes he took playful ways of reproving or trying to put matters right when he thought it needful. The following letter to his brother-in-law, Mr. William Dickson, will explain itself :—

'" *Fields of Ephratah*,"
Summer-days of A.D. 1872.

'MR. EDITOR,—I find in my peregrinations, that not a few, both ministers and people, who take a deep interest in the Sabbath school, are annually brought into straits and difficulties at the S.S. Breakfast. They complain that they neither can get a good supply for the body, nor hear comfortably (there being almost no room for sitting), so as to get their spirit refreshed. They suggest that a larger ' Upper Room' should somewhere be found. The Master's Upper Room seems to have been large and airy—at least held comfortably all who came. Excuse me troubling you with this note, but you are understood to be most willing to take any suggestion that may help on the cause, and promote the interests of the young.—Yours in the common faith and hope,   A FELLOW-LABOURER.'

He was at one time troubled by some of the people coming in late to church. As he was reading and commenting on the tenth chapter of Acts one afternoon, he came to the verse : ' Now therefore are we all here present before God.' He stopped and said, ' I think that is more than some of us could have said this morning !' Another time he said, ' A great many were late this morning—not like Mary Magdalene, *early* at the sepulchre.'

His candour and straightforwardness sometimes made

him appear unsympathetic, for he never tried to please any one at the expense of truth. 'There are some people who can stand anything but flattery. If no one ever praises you, you are all the better for it!' After the meeting in 1888 to celebrate his 'Jubilee,' an old Collace friend remarked to him that it had been a 'grand meeting.' He replied, 'Yes, but I think there was too much praise of man, and too little to God. I never thought I did more than draw the water and let the flock drink.'

The story with which he closed his address on that same evening was one which he often told in illustration of what humbles a minister, and delivers him from self-satisfaction.

A Grecian painter had executed a remarkable painting of a boy carrying on his head a basket of grapes. So exquisitely were the grapes painted, that when the picture was put up in the Forum for the admiration of the citizens, the birds pecked the grapes, thinking they were real. The friends of the painter were full of congratulations, but he did not seem at all satisfied. When they asked him why, he replied, 'I should have done a great deal more. I should have painted the boy so true to life that the birds would not have dared to come near!'

MANSE MEMORIES

' Paul is like a man climbing a mountain,—sometimes on an eminence and in the bright sunshine, sometimes down in a shady hollow, sometimes wrapped in mist and gloom,—but always singing !'—*A. A. B.*

CHAPTER VII

AT the beginning of his ministry Dr. Bonar said in one of his letters: 'This is a time that seems to require prayer more than preaching even, at least so I often feel. And persevering prayerfulness — day by day wrestling and pleading—is harder for the flesh than preaching.'

As years passed the 'main business of every day' to him was prayer, and latterly, when overwhelmed by work,—visits, letters, interruptions, engagements of every kind,—it was his rule to devote two hours every day, before going out, to prayer and meditation on God's Word. When the settlement of his colleague, Mr. M'Intyre, in 1891, had relieved him of some of his former duties, his Sabbath evenings were spent in prayer in his study. A card hung on one side of his mantelpiece on which were printed the words, ' *Dimidium studii qui rite precatur habet*,'—' He who has truly prayed has completed the half of his study.' Early visitors to his study in India Street were familiar with the sight of his figure standing at his desk writing letters, as was his habit always after breakfast. In the afternoon he visited regularly from one o'clock till nearly five, and every evening was filled up with a meeting of some kind. Friday and Saturday were kept as days of preparation for Sabbath, and no visitor was admitted to his study on Saturday unless his errand were of great

importance. One who had much intercourse with him
in work had occasion to call on a Friday afternoon
when he was busy with his preparation for the pulpit.
He appeared like one lost to himself in communion
with God, and the visitor left, feeling overawed. Like
John Bunyan in his dream, he had seen a man ' with
his eyes lifted up to Heaven, the best of books in his
hand, the law of truth written upon his lips, and the
world behind his back.'

His study-hours during the week were constantly
interrupted, and it was sometimes difficult to see how
preparation for his many meetings and classes was ever
accomplished. ' There were many coming and going,
and they had no leisure so much as to eat,' was sometimes literally true in his experience. Yet he never
went to his own pulpit or to a meeting unprepared,
and he spoke often of the necessity of first receiving
a blessing ourselves from the subject to be spoken of,
before giving out to others.

' Use for yourself first what the Lord teaches you,
and if He spare you, use it for others.'

' When you have got a blessing, take time to let it
sink into your own heart before you tell it out.'

It was a favourite thought of his that when a blessing
is got from the Lord, part of it is to be given away.
' There is " *seed for the sower*," ' he used to say, ' as well
as " bread for the eater." ' He spoke of Psalm xxiii. 5 :
' " My cup runneth over." He filled it, and then poured
in more ! Stop ! No, let somebody else get a share.
He gave me an overflow for the sake of others.'

His splendid constitution, his vigour of body, added
to his regular habits and his great calmness of mind,
made possible for him what few other men could have
attempted. Often he referred with thankfulness to the
unbroken sleep he enjoyed at night. In his study he

was at home, and every corner of it spoke of himself,
everything in perfect order—no book or paper ever out
of its place. 'Untidiness,' he used to say, 'is un-
christian.' His Bible always lay on the table, and his
Hebrew Bible and little Greek Testament on a small
table by the fireplace. Till his eyesight began to fail
slightly, he used a very old Bible of his father's which
he valued much. On its blank pages are written shorthand notes of his conversations with his old minister,
Dr. Jones, when he joined the Church in 1830, and
other jottings from sermons of his which had impressed
him. On another page he has written these lines in
shorthand :—

> 'Behold the book whose leaves display
> Jesus the Life, the Truth, the Way ;
> Read it with diligence and care,
> Search it, for thou shalt find Him there.'

In his study hung the text he was so fond of, and
had had printed for himself : '*But Thou remainest.*' A
lady called to see him one day, in great sorrow and
depression of mind. Nothing seemed to bring her any
comfort. All at once, as they talked together, Dr.
Bonar saw her face light up, and she said, 'You don't
need to say anything more. I have got what I need ;'
and she pointed to the words of the text which had
caught her eye : '*But Thou remainest.*' He used to recall often a scene in his study, when a working-man came
one evening to see him in great distress about his soul.
During their conversation the light broke in upon him,
and, striking his hand on his knee, the man exclaimed,
'I never all my life expected to have joy like this !'

One of the treasures of his study was a piece of
Samuel Rutherford's pulpit, which always lay on the
mantelpiece. Another much-prized relic was a panel of
Lady Kenmure's pew in Anwoth Church. His reverence

for everything connected with the saints of former times was well known, and was often a subject of playful raillery on the part of his friends.

When in America, in the summer of 1881, he visited Northampton, out of love for the memory of Jonathan Edwards and David Brainerd, and wrote to his daughter at home :—

'*Northfield*, 23*rd Aug.* 1881.

'MY DEAR MARJORY,—I have been taking a quiet walk among shrubs and pines on the slope of a hill, and the little burn gave me opportunity to sit down and work away, making waterfalls, etc., as if in Arran or in Mull.

'On Saturday last, Isabella and I, with Major Whittle, Emma Moody, and a nice old minister from Philadelphia, made out a visit to Northampton, the town of Jonathan Edwards. You know how much I desired to be there, and our visit was most interesting. But we missed you, for there were some views which would have afforded you grand work for your pencil. We sat under, and climbed so far up, the two old elm-trees planted in front of his house by Jonathan Edwards, and I can *sell* you, when I return, a piece of the bark ! You will have to sketch from my rude materials Brainerd's tomb, which we next visited, and some other gravestones, full of interest. The old church, the scene of the great Revivals, was burnt many years ago.'

In his diary he wrote, in a different strain, his reflections and feelings in connection with this visit :—

'I bless the Lord for this day with all its sacred memories, "Is the Spirit of the Lord straitened ?" Is not Jesus Christ the same yesterday, to-day, and for ever ? Father, Thou hast brought me at this time of my life across the sea, to stand at this spot, and there pray and call to mind "the days of the right hand of the Most High." Surely Thou hast in store very much blessing for me and my people and my land ! Come as near, come in the revelation of the same glorious holiness as to Thy servants then.'

And next day, Sabbath, August 21st, he writes :—

'Much stirred up by yesterday's visit to Northampton, and the train of thought and prayer it led to. . . . Lord, give me fully what is meant by "that Christ may dwell in your heart," and by

" Christ liveth in me." I preached on Isa. liii. 2, but did not feel [helped]. I fear that yesterday, having got a full cup, I did not set it down before the Lord on the mercy-seat with thanks and praise, and with the appeal, Eph. iii. 20-21.'

Many a journey he made to spots of historic interest, and he would go any distance to see the grave of a martyr, or the home of a saint of God. In 1860 he made a pilgrimage through Dumfriesshire and Kirkcudbrightshire along with Mr. James Crawford of Edinburgh, and wrote to Mrs. Bonar during their wanderings :—

' *Kirkcudbright, 2nd August* 1860.—Of course we made a pilgrimage to the churchyard and its martyrs' graves, accompanied by a very intelligent policeman who knows some Latin, and helped us to read the tombstones and search for the grave of Marion M'Naught.[1] We did not succeed in finding this grave, but we found the site of her house where Samuel Rutherford used to call. It is just coming down to make way for another, so I brought away a stone of it ! That stone must have sent back the sound of the voices of both Samuel Rutherford and Marion M'Naught, as well as of Blair when his horse stopped at the door, and he found his two friends ready to give him a welcome.'

On this journey he wrote one of his amusing letters to his brother John, dated from Anwoth, and purporting to be from Samuel Rutherford :—

' *3rd August* 1860.

'SWEET AND WORTHY BROTHER,—You did well some years ago to visit the scenes of my former labours. Did you not agree with me in calling the swallows that build their nests at Anwoth Church, "blessed birds"? I see two of your friends have this summer come to tread in your steps—one of them is a younger brother of yours, the other writes after his name, Eccl. Scot. Lib. E.C. There was no such church in my day, but I always said that Scotland's sky would clear again. And I dow [2] declare that, if only they will go home more prayerful than they came, this visit to Anwoth will not have been in vain. But, perhaps, dearest and truly-honoured brother, you would like to know a little about

---

[1] One of Rutherford's correspondents, the wife of the Provost of Kirkcudbright.

[2] Can, am able ; frequently used in Rutherford's *Letters*.

their journey. Let me tell you, therefore, that they came by way of Kirkcudbright. While there they sought out the house of Marion M'Naught. This generation (who are never long content with what their fathers did) are at this moment pulling that dwelling down ; but your two friends have picked out of the crumbling lime a piece of stone (which no doubt they will send to you) which must have echoed back my loud burst of surprise and joy on that memorable night when Robert Blair, my fellow-prisoner and true servant to his master, came from Ireland straight to Marion M'Naught's dwelling. They have been away at her tomb also, which is marked by a flat stone near the spot where two martyrs lie waiting for the Day of Resurrection. I may tell you, besides, that they set out for Dundrennan Abbey, where that idol-loving Queen Mary took refuge for a night. Dear and trusty brother, I was not in the way of going aside to see even broken idols, and, if I mistake not, neither are you. Your friends did far better next day when they visited Borgue and sought out the old house of my friend the Laird of Roberton, Carleton also, and Knock-brex, all men of God, men who would own no hireling for their pastor, and who lodged Christ when others would give Him no roof for His head. They have this afternoon been looking down on Cardoness, and Cally, and Rusco, and Ardwell, as well as walking up my "Walk." If they might only walk in my steps so far as I tried to be Caleb-like ! I persuade myself that it is so far well for this generation that they built a monument to me, inas-much as it was not to myself (if I dow think and say this), but to the cause which I ever loved and defended. Your brother is reported to be about to preach in Anwoth on the coming Sabbath. This will be all well if only he preach Him who is worthy to be praised, and so worthy to be preached, and if he will cry up that Plant of Renown, in spite of unwilling hearts, that love to hear the news of a passing-away world.

'I should perhaps advise them to visit Wigtown, and to go home-ward by Glenkens. O Earlston ! Earlston ! ye stood fast and well in the day of battle.

'But I have written too much. I hold my peace here. Remember my love to your wife, and say that she has the good wishes of one who signs himself,—Your unworthy brother,

S. R.'

He often amused himself by writing in this strain, and he and his brothers exchanged many such letters.

From Haworth, in Yorkshire, he wrote again to his brother John :—

> ' *Not far from Haworth,*
> 15*th July* 1878.

'DEAR AND HONOURED BROTHER,—Some years ago (was it not in 1867 ?) you kindly visited my church and resting-place, though I myself had gone away to the "mountain of myrrh" to spend a few days there with Wesley and Whitefield and John Berridge "till the day break." It seems that a brother of yours has called at Haworth on the same brotherly errand. He heard the clatter of the pattens which the people here use, old and young, and he saw the place in sunshine, when it looks pretty well. He could not fail to notice "The Black Bull" and "The White Lion," public-houses near my church, out of which (when the windows were nearer the ground than now) I often chased drinkers and loungers found there after service began, and you would have smiled to see the haste they made to escape by window or door. Your brother stood on my resting-place ; you know it is marked by no inscription, but the slab that covers my bones is right in front of the Brontés' grand tablet on the wall. . . . The old house where I lived is the old piece of the present parsonage, and your brother reverently walked along the track in the churchyard by which I used to go down from the house that was my abode to the House of God. He went up to my pulpit, too, and how could I help wishing that he may yet see in the pews of his own church as many weeping eyes and bowed-down heads as I often saw all over these seats ! But do you know that they are going to pull down this church and build a new and larger one ? I am almost sorry—though what is a building but a platform erected in order to get the true stones hoisted up into their places? Your brother (is he quite free from that reverence for holy spots which Stephen, in Acts vii., shows to be no part of worship *?)* was overheard asking the schoolmaster if he knew where "the clerk's house" stood, in which I was once prostrated by an overwhelming discovery of divine grace and glory. But that house is long since removed ; it was a mere room near the church for the clerk's use. He was asking, too, for the place where I began to know the Lord—Todmorden ; the people often call it "Tommorden." It is ten or twelve miles from Haworth, as you know.

' But I daresay you are tired with this long epistle, as your brother was when he got back that night to Keighley. So I bid

you heartily farewell, not doubting to meet you some day in brighter sunshine than Haworth ever knew.—Your brother,
'WILLIAM GRIMSHAW.'

Another letter of this kind he wrote on the occasion of his brother's 'Jubilee' at Greenock in 1885 :—

'*Paradise, the Third Heavens.*

'DEAR AND HONOURED BROTHER,—I cannot be present in body at your jubilee next week, being detained a willing prisoner in the King's Palace here; but I send my loving salutations, and hope you are in good case, albeit ye be sometimes wechted with your fourscore and two years. I know ye handle the pen of a ready writer, but, for all that, it may be weel for you to look into ye buik I send you, to wit, some old sermons of mine, which ye may preach when ye run dry. It seems you were ordained in 1835. Now, two hundred years before that (1635) there was a dial[1] or horologe set up in the garden of my Lady Kenmure by an ancestor of yours. Ye have seen it, and read on its face, "Joannes Bonar, fecit."

'Hoping to meet you in Immanuel's Land when the great jubilee trumpe shall be blown,—Your very loving brother,
'SAMUEL RUTHERFORD.
'Misspend not your short sandglass, which runneth very fast.'

During the sittings of the General Assembly in 1882, he spent a day in visiting Ormiston and other places of interest. He describes it thus to Mr. Manson :—

'You will have been visited, I suppose, by some of my family in search of primroses and spring flowers. Meanwhile, their father has been doing duty (1) as a preacher of the Word at Lanark on Sabbath; (2) as an ecclesiastic; (3) as a lover of good men, such as John Knox and George Wishart, on (if not *in*) whose footsteps he was treading yesterday. For you must know that, while the brethren were battering the crumbling walls of the "Estab-lishment," I did yesterday go on pilgrimage. I set out with Mr. Glendinning, who knows all that region, to visit some localities of interest in Midlothian. We saw where Knox and

---

[1] When walking in the grounds of Kenmure Castle one day, Dr. John Bonar and a friend who was with him had their attention drawn to an old sun-dial in the garden. After carefully scraping away the moss which had gathered over it, they read the inscription, 'Joannes Bonar fecit !'

Wishart took their last farewell of each other, and the large (the largest in Scotland) yew-tree under which Wishart preached. This was at Ormiston House. It was very interesting, also, to stand on high ground and look around. Yonder is Saltoun where Fletcher the statesman lived. . . . There, yonder, is Pencaitland, where, in old days, Calderwood was minister. . . . But—I must off to the Assembly.'

'Scotland will never know,' he said, 'till the Great Day, what it owes to its martyrs' prayers, when they lay for days and months hidden in the moors and caves. God put them there on purpose.'

In his friend, the Rev. J. H. Thomson of Hightae, he found a sympathetic and enthusiastic co-worker in the field of covenanting lore, and during fifteen years he kept up a constant correspondence with him on subjects relating to the Reformers and the Martyrs. When editing an edition of the *Scots Worthies* and when preparing both *Letters* and *Sermons of Samuel Rutherford* for the press, Mr. Thomson was his unfailing referee. Sometimes he addresses him as 'My dear Interpreter,' 'My dear Zaphnath-paaneah' (*see* margin, Gen. xli. 45), 'My dear Philo-Rhaetorfortis,' or 'Amice foederatorum.'

'Glean more and more in the fields of Bethlehem,' he writes, 'and, when you please, "let fall of purpose handfuls for me."'

'There is something about Alexander Peden's sermons that takes me more than almost any man of that time. I wish we had more of him.'

'Peace be with you. May the people of Hightae find that their minister comes in for a large share of the answer to the martyrs' prayer.'

At the close of a letter, in reference to the transcription of some sermons of Samuel Rutherford which Mr. Thomson had undertaken, Dr. Bonar says :—

'Should you not preach to your people what you find so

satisfying to your own soul in Samuel Rutherford?—Yours truly, dear Interpreter, who gives out to pilgrims things "rare" if not wonderful.'

At other times he signs himself, ' Yours truly in Him who ever hears the cry, Rev. vi. 10'; ' Yours truly in Him who cares for the dust of Zion more than any of us do.'

' In July 1880,' Mr. Thomson writes, ' Dr. Bonar came to assist at the dispensation of the Lord's Supper at Hightae. It was a visit much to be remembered. He was in full vigour of mind and body, and gave no less than five addresses, perhaps the best being his sermon to the children on Sabbath afternoon. On the Tuesday we started on a long-promised expedition to the Enterkin Pass. The morning was fair, but as we got near Elvanfoot drops of rain gave ominous warning of the showers that afterwards overtook us. At Elvanfoot we got the mail-gig for Leadhills. The driver at once recognised Dr. Bonar, and showed us no little kindness, walking with us across the moor after reaching Leadhills, until we came to the head of the pass, where the ground is about 700 feet above the level of the sea. The road down the pass no longer exists. It has been washed away, and in its place there remains only the loose shingle on the hillside that runs down to the ravine below, in which rushes along the Enterkin Burn. It was not easy to keep one's footing on the loose pebbles, but Dr. Bonar went along with the agility and confidence of a born mountaineer until we came to the foot of the pass, where the prisoners were rescued from the soldiers by their Covenanting friends. Though the rain fell heavily as we came down the pass, his cheerfulness never flagged, and he discussed the possibilities of Defoe's graphic account of the rescue with all the interest of one familiar with the story from his early days. . . . Dr. Bonar spoke much as he wrote. A genial humour ran through his conversation. He loved to express himself quaintly, but it was always as a Christian scholar whose chief study was the Bible, and one of whose leading aims was to tell about its treasures to others. His delight in the Reformers and Covenanters, and especially in Samuel Rutherford, arose very much from the conviction that their chief study and chief aims were like his own. Communion with the saints was, therefore, a leading characteristic of his life. It gave directness to his studies and a charm to his conversation.'

Dr. Bonar liked to trace a family connection with good Colonel Gardiner, and Mrs. Bonar claimed kindred with James Renwick the martyr. The Greyfriars' Churchyard in Edinburgh was a favourite haunt of his, and many a friend did he take to see the martyrs' grave and the stone where the Covenant was signed. He loved his native town, and was always glad when occasion led him back to Edinburgh. In one of his letters he tells of an amusing interview with a cabman soon after coming to Glasgow. When he had paid his fare, the man looked at him with a half-smile, and said, ' Sir, you micht gie me anither saxpence, for we 're baith Edinburgh men !'

The earliest recollection of his childhood was the firing of the Castle guns in 1815 to celebrate the victory of Waterloo. He often went to look at the old house in Paterson's Court, Broughton, where he was born on the 29th of May 1810, and where his early years were spent. His home was a bright and happy one, where family affection and healthy enjoyments went side by side with simple piety. To their early training all the family owed in great part their thorough knowledge of the Bible and of the Shorter Catechism, and the stores of paraphrases and hymns which they held in their memory. Andrew was the youngest boy, and was always quiet and studious. His first literary effort was a ' History of the Rabbits,' which he wrote when he was eleven years old. The gentleness and modesty which became so characteristic of the man were early apparent in the boy. On the day on which he gained the Dux Gold Medal of the High School in 1825 he came home as usual, and said nothing about it till his mother asked at the dinner-table, 'Well, Andrew, and who got the Gold Medal to-day?' when he quietly drew it out of his pocket. The death of his father in

1821 was the first event which left an impression on his mind, and he very often referred to it.

When his son was spending a summer session in Edinburgh, in 1872, he wrote to him :—

'Do you ever look along at the spot where your father and grandfather, uncles, and aunts used to encamp? Only think, it is half a century now since the day when your grandfather was carried to his last resting-place in the Canongate Churchyard from Paterson's Court.'

'You congratulate me on my birthday being at hand. . . . To you and your sisters I send my hearty thanks and my prayer that if you be spared as long as I have been since first I drew breath near where you now are, in one of the rooms of that pillared house in Paterson's Court, you all may have enjoyed as much as I have done of the "glorious Gospel of the blessed God," through which we find communion with God restored.'

After a visit to Edinburgh and to the house in 24 Gayfield Square, which had been his home at another time, he writes to Mrs. Bonar :—

'I saw the room we studied in so long, and *where I remember first of realising a found Saviour.*'

When the Queen came to Edinburgh on one occasion, he took his two youngest daughters with him to see her. As they were walking about, they met his old friend, Mr. Walker of Perth, and Dr. Bonar said to him, 'You see I've brought my children in to see the Queen.' 'Very good,' was Mr. Walker's reply. 'Yes,' said Dr. Bonar, 'we saw her, but we were not changed ; but "when we see *Him* we shall be *like* Him."'

The summer holidays were always spent with his family in the country or by the sea. He was much attached to the East Coast, associated as it was with his early recollections, but many of his summers were spent among the wilder and grander scenery of the West Highlands. One of his letters to Mr. Manson

from Mull, in the summer of 1882, records a visit to
Iona to which he often looked back with great interest:—

'*Graignure, 25th August* 1880.

'MY DEAR FRIEND,—I returned from Iona last night, having
spent five days in that region. Our Sabbath (the Communion)
was a delightful day; outwardly all was still, calm, and bright
sunshine, the sea smooth as if it had been of crystal, and as to the
inward work we had the deepest attention and solemnity. While
Mr. Blacklock conducted in Gaelic the forenoon opening services
under the blue sky on the "field of the Druids" (the last of the
Druids are said to be buried there), I took the services in the
church. After the first Table, we who were English-speaking
came out to the open air and gave place to the Gaelic worshippers
who then sat down at the Table. We had with us a sample of "the
Great Multitude from all nations," for there were with us a United
Presbyterian minister (Robertson of Irvine), an Episcopalian minister from Norfolkshire, the Established Church minister of Glen-
urquhart, and an English Presbyterian from Liverpool, while Mr.
Blacklock represented the country, and I the town. As we crossed
and re-crossed the Sound to get to the Manse, those in the boat
kept singing praise.

'By the bye, the wife of an old elder here paid me as great a
compliment as was once paid to you in Rannoch. She said that
my English was well understood by the Gaelic people, for "it was
not grammatical!"[1] Tell me all you discover of Covenanting
times—Carsphairn is redolent with such memories. . . . Janie is
going to supplement my letter, so tha I may close, subscribing
my name.

I am A. A. B.
As you at once see;
Sojourning in Mull,
And trying to cull
Sermons from stones
And Culdee bones!'

Another letter gives a glimpse of his employments in
the Highlands :—

'On Sabbath I was sailing across the Sound of Mull to preach
at Loch Aline. The sea was like the "sea of glass" in the Apoca-

---

[1] The old woman's exact words were, 'We understand you, for you have
no grammar!'

lypse, so that you see if you had a snatch of " Paradise," I had a
glimpse of the " New Earth." . . . We have a good deal of bio-
graphy with us ; some poetry, a little Latin, and German and
French and Hebrew.   Very miscellaneous, you may well suppose.
All this is an appendix to the Book of Nature, which we came here
to study.'

Besides reading and walking, his holiday occupations
were varied by occasional hours of hoeing and weeding.
Nettles and dandelions were mercilessly attacked, generally by his umbrella for want of a better weapon, and
every paper on the pathway had to be cleared away.
Some of his friends professed to let their gardens lie
waste in expectation of his annual visits.   He had a
great horror of an untidy manse-garden, and used to
remind the owner that 'æsthetics are next to ethics.'
When visiting an old friend in Dumfriesshire he wrote
home saying he was busy putting the garden in order,
and added :—

> ' If you want a field of labour
> You will find it anywhere ! '

His favourite poets, Milton and Cowper, were generally his companions in the country.   He delighted in
sacred poetry, and read and often quoted Montgomery's
Hymns, the Olney *Hymns*, and Hart's *Hymns*.   Though
he found it difficult to quote any of these correctly
in the pulpit, he could repeat easily and fluently any
of Dr. Watts' well-known hymns, which he had learned
from his mother in his childhood.   Sometimes on a
Sabbath evening, when his day's work was over, he
would read aloud or have his children read to him,
passages from Baxter's *Saints' Rest*, or Rutherford's
Letters, or Ambrose's *Looking unto Jesus*, or John
Bunyan's story of the pilgrims crossing the river.
Latin and English classics, etymology, and topography
were his recreations.   His reading was extremely careful
and minute, and he had a knack of picking out what-

ever in a book was noteworthy, though he seemed to
have only read it hurriedly. In taking up a volume
out of his library one turns involuntarily to the blank
leaf at the end to see what is marked there as specially
interesting. His comments are written freely and are
sometimes amusing. A book written many years ago
by a Moderate minister has this note: 'Moderatism
sometimes points out the moral lessons well, but oftener
shows how to overlook the true sense.' At the end of
his copy of Marshall *on Sanctification*, he has written:
'There is real endowment for holiness wherever justification has taken place, even if little felt. But the best
endowment is not only the fact of justification but also
the knowledge of that fact.' On a copy of Faber's
Hymns which he gave to his daughter he wrote: 'On
her birthday. With the apostle's caution, 1 John iv. 1.'
He added the following note to a volume of sermons
which he sent to his son: 'Poison; to be taken in
small doses and to be used along with what Christiana
got for her boy in the House Beautiful from Mr. Skill,
a purge made *ex carne et sanguine Christi.*'

The Hebrew and Greek Testaments were his constant
study, and he used to ask young ministers when they
came to see him, ' Do you still keep up your Greek and
Hebrew?' If they hesitated or said 'no,' he would say,
'Read one verse in Greek and Hebrew every day and
you will be surprised how it will help you.' He is
remembered in his student days as stirring others up
to a proper study of Hebrew, and no other student of
his time had an equal talent for languages. He was
remarkable for his diligence and improvement of time,
and for his indomitable energy. Nothing that he tried
to master baffled him except singing, which he was
never able to acquire. His great desire was to learn
even one tune, that he might be able to help at a
meeting or sing by a sick-bed, but he never succeeded.

Naturally shy and reserved, he was the life of any company where he felt at home, and he had the charm of perfect naturalness, and an entire want of self-consciousness. The continual sunshine in which he lived made him attractive to both old and young, and his humour, instead of decreasing, grew more intense as he grew older. One of his friends remarked of his home life that it was a new illustration of the truth that wisdom's ways 'are ways of pleasantness, and all her paths are peace.' His letters to his children are brimming over with fun, intermingled with the most serious and loving words. As birthdays came round he always made reference to them at family worship. 'Bless the one of our number whose birthday this is. May this be a day for heavenly favours and heavenly gifts.' One of his daughters said one morning with a sigh, 'I am a quarter of a century old to-day.' Immediately he rejoined, 'You have reached half your jubilee!' On a card, which he sent as a birthday greeting to his youngest daughter, he wrote :—

> 'Better and wiser every day,
> Till every hair on your head be gray !'

His family had presented him with a reading-lamp on his birthday, and he expressed his thanks in the following letter to his daughter, then in London :—

. . . 'Hoping to see you very soon, I write to-day merely to acknowledge your gift on my birthday—for I understand all of you joined in it. It was very kind and mindful in you all. I began a poem on the occasion, but the muse deserted me very soon. Here is the fragment, however :

> 'A son and daughters four of mine
> Resolved together to combine
>   Their father to enlighten—
> That so there might be nothing found
> Within his study, all around,
>   To startle or affrighten.'

Good-bye,—Your affectionate father,   ANDREW A. BONAR.

Many years ago when at Collace he sent to a friend of Mrs. Bonar's in Edinburgh before her wedding, the following

'HEADS OF MARRIAGE SERVICE

To be delivered when Miss W—— becomes Mrs. Y——

I. Your past experience. *N. B.*—The wide field of unmarried life.

II. Your prospects as they appear to cool and impartial and thoughtful friends.

III. Your imaginary discovery of a complete continent of excellences in each other.

IV. Your sober realisation of each other's faults, failures, follies, etc.

V. The question—will you now proceed? Yes or No. Speak audibly and without faltering.'

His postcards were often a source of amusement to his friends. The following one was sent to Dr. Somerville as an apology for not being present at a meeting :—

' 20 *India Street, Saturday.*

Ἀδελφέ μοῦ ἀγαπητέ,

Necesse est me adire Greenock hodie, quia crastino die οἱ μαθῆται συνάγονται κλάσαι ἄρτον.

Saludad á todos hermanos. La gracia sea con todos vosotros.

ANDREW A BONAR. הָרֹעֶה בְּפְנָחַסְתִּן

From Northfield he wrote in 1881 to his youngest daughter :—

' MY DEAR MARY,—What a country this is ! They give us curry and beefsteaks to breakfast, and potatoes and squash and doughnuts ! At dinner we often get sokotash, a mixture of Indian corn and beans. A large bird (more than twice the size of our red-robin) comes morning by morning to the field before my window to get worms, and it is the American robin-redbreast. We have pine-trees instead of fir-trees.

' But I 'll tell you two or three things I do not quite like, though everybody here is as kind as possible. One is, their roads—not kept in good repair either in town or country. Another is, the people do not bring Bibles with them to the church, nor do they sing the Psalms.   And still another—the Sabbath-school children in their churches do not learn a catechism-lesson.   They are far behind us in all these things, so that I like our own land after all, and shall be glad to return.   I hope to find you wonderfully improved, body, soul, and spirit.—Your affectionate father,

'ANDREW A. BONAR.'

Another letter to his son is a playful criticism of his book, *Letters of Ricardo to Malthus.*

'*Glasgow, 25th November* 1887.

'MY DEAR JAMES,—It seems to me that you have edited the *Letters of Ricardo to Malthus* with great skill, and evidently with great care.   I have no doubt that your book will be very interesting to all students of Political Economy, giving the private discussion (so to speak) of the great subject by two such men as Ricardo and Malthus.   Cobbett's bitterness (at p. 162, note) in criticising Malthus is the raciest part of the book. . . .

FOR MARY (MRS. BONAR)

'Notice at p. 45, "Mrs. Ricardo, standing by me, has made me express myself in a more than usually bungling manner."

'*Inference.* Never stand near Dr. James when he is writing.

'At p. 54, a certain lady, Mrs. Smith, asks Ricardo to procure for her some letter of Malthus.   In reply he says, "Knowing that I had many which would not discredit you, I assented."

'*Query.* If any friend should ask me for such a specimen letter of Dr. James Bonar could I say, "Having many which would not discredit him"?   I could send one letter of three sentences, another of two, I believe !

'At p. 240, might not the editor when mentioning "Huish, near Chippenham," have added in a parenthesis ["Chippenham ! where the little church stands in which J. B. and M. M. were united in holy matrimony."]

'One great defect occurs at the very outset.   You have not written my name on it. . . . I go to-morrow to open a new church at Scone, where Scotland's kings used to be crowned.   I think I must bid the congregation remember the "King of kings," singing

"Bring forth the royal diadem,
And crown *Him* Lord of all !"

—Your affectionate father,   A. A. B.

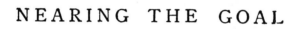

NEARING THE GOAL

'Who but a Christian through all life
    That blessing may prolong?
Who, through the world's sad day of strife
    Still chant his morning song?'

'Ever the richest, tenderest glow
    Sets round the autumnal sun ;
But there sight fails : no heart may know
    The bliss when life is done !'

KEBLE.

CHAPTER VIII

IT was not only to the saints of other days that his affection was drawn out, but his love for the brethren was shown in his deep and lasting attachment to those who enjoyed his closer friendship, and to others whom he knew little, but loved because they loved the Lord. He believed in the communion of saints, and one of his chief regrets at the abolition of the Fast-Days preparatory to the observance of the Lord's Supper, was the loss of the brotherly fellowship which was always enjoyed at these times. Speaking one day of hermits he described them as 'earthworms,' and said, 'a man can't meditate when he is always alone. He needs to have intercourse with others to stir him up to meditation.' 'When are we to meet?' he writes to a friend. 'Sometimes it seems to me to be true of *meetings* what Arnauld said of *rest*: 'We shall *meet* in eternity. O day of glory! O day of our gathering together in Him!' 'Are you not saddened by Spurgeon's illness?' he writes to another friend. 'What can we say but Ezekiel xi. 13, and sing "God lives! bless'd be my Rock!" The friends of other days, and those whom he regarded as his own children in the faith, were very near his heart. His love for the Jews, begun so early in life, continued unabated to the end. Anything connected with them or their land was to him of peculiar interest. Next to the joyful hope of the King Himself on the throne was

the thought of a restored nation worshipping at His feet,
and a land to which had been given back 'the beauty
of Lebanon and the excellency of Carmel and Sharon.'
Nothing was more gladdening to his heart than the
news of one and another of the sons of Israel being
brought into the fold of Christ. Writing to Dr. J. H.
Wilson, regarding the baptism of a Jew which was to
take place in the Barclay Church, Edinburgh, he says :—

'We shall try to remember you on Sabbath when you expect
to baptize C——.   A branch of the "old olive-tree" will be
waving in your church in the person of these two sons of Abraham.
May you find peculiar blessing on yourself and on your people !'

To another friend he writes :—

'I anticipate great pleasure from meeting with Mr. S. We
must get good olive oil from him, he is a berry of the good olive-
tree' (Rom. xi. 24).

An amusing interview took place between Mr. Rabbinovitch and himself in a friend's house. Mr. Rabbinovitch rose from his chair to offer it to Dr. Bonar as he
came into the room. He tried to prevent him from rising
and said, 'No, no, *to the Jew first*!' Mr. Rabbinovitch
replied, 'But thou shalt rise up before the face of the
old man !'

Often in later years he refers in his letters to those
who have passed away from the old circle of friends.
'You notice William Burns must have got over the river,
and in at the gate of the Celestial City a month at least
before John Milne. Well, he and Milne and Patrick
Miller, and Robert M'Cheyne, and James Hamilton,
have been talking over the past.'

'Did you notice Dr. Keith's death [1880]? in a good
old age—eighty-nine—like the Patriarchs. He has gone
on to "New Jerusalem," and soon probably the last of

the four who in 1839 travelled Palestine together, may make up to him. Oh, it will be glorious to stand within the gates of ' Jerusalem that cometh down from heaven,' and to see the King in His beauty in His own land— Immanuel's Land ! '

' I have been thinking that saints certainly remember those they left behind, and are certainly looking forward to the day of "our gathering together in Him " ; but they do not miss us as we miss them.'

Christians of all denominations were his friends, and many who differed widely from him in opinion loved him with a deep affection. He liked to remind believers of their duty to all saints, and the blessedness of united prayer and united effort.

' In holiness we must go on together, not alone. You will not get on by separating yourself to read and pray. It must be " along with them that call on the Lord." We are to climb Pisgah together, and from the top see the stretch of the land. But we are not to go alone.' ' God loves unity, and so He loves a united cry, a petition signed by more than one.' ' Christ liked to come to the feast when He was going to give blessing. He liked to come to the upper room when they were all assembled there.'

He was firm in adherence to his own principles, and those who did not know him well had no idea of the determined force of will that lay beneath his gentle kindliness. Independent in word and action to the last degree, what others might think or say of him was to him of no consequence. Occasionally his determination was almost provoking, and yet, in the end, it had often to be admitted that he was right ! The nickname of ' Old Obstinate,' which his friend Mr. Patrick Miller of Newcastle gave to him in early days, stuck to him to the last. ' " Who sweareth (engageth) to his own hurt and changeth not," is sometimes a troublesome text to a man's conscience,' he wrote to a friend who in vain had begged him to change his plans. Another time he wrote :—

'I could not be away another Sabbath for a long time. It not only interrupts the begun chain of ordinary lecture, etc., but it disturbs (1) my Young Men's Class ; (2) My visits to the Sabbath-school (which I could not even last Sabbath commence) ; (3) My evening prayer-meeting ; (4) My own equanimity !'

A Presbyterian to the backbone [1] and a loyal Free Churchman, his sympathies, in latter years especially, went out far beyond his own church. He loved the gatherings together of God's people, and in the Conferences at Mildmay, at Perth, in his own city, and in many other places, his presence and his words were an inspiration.

On one occasion, when addressing the Mildmay Conference, he spoke of the Old Testament saints as being not inferior givers to the saints of the New Testament. He referred to Moses being commanded by God during the erection of the Tabernacle to stop the people from giving more, and quaintly threw in the remark, 'I don't find it necessary to do this when I go to the country to preach for a collection at the opening of a new church!' 'There is a chapter,' he said, 'one of the longest in the Bible, that I don't believe any one here has read all through. It is the seventh of Numbers. It tells that one of the princes of Israel wished to give a gift to God, and asked Moses if he might. Moses did not want to answer of his own accord, and so he asked God. God said, " Let him give it. He will like to do it, and you will lay it out on a table "—just as brides do with their wedding gifts to show how their friends love them.

---

[1] While his son was at Oxford he wrote to him : ' How do you get on with the Thirty-Nine Articles ? They are good and sound—all except that about bishops,' etc.

The prince gave a silver bowl filled with the finest of the wheat, and a golden spoon. The next day another prince came with the same request, and brought the same gift, and all the princes of the twelve tribes did the same. David, at his death, bequeathed to the Lord's service more gold than is contained in the Bank of England,[1] besides what he had given during his lifetime. In the New Testament we read of one Joseph or Joses, surnamed Barnabas, who sold his estate in Cyprus and gave the price of it to the Lord. On one occasion Paul and he were on a missionary tour in Cyprus, and one afternoon Barnabas proposed that they should take a walk together, and said, "If you like to come with me I will show you the estate that I sold and gave to the Lord." So they went together, and when Paul saw it he said, "Barnabas, what a beautiful place this is! It must have cost you many a pang before you sold it. Do you never grudge having done it?" "Never," said Barnabas, "the Lord has made all up to me, and more. Men never call me Joses now; it is always 'Barnabas, the son of consolation.'"'

In giving an address at the Perth Conference upon 'Faith' he supposed some of the later disciples saying to each other, 'Come, let us go to the apostle John and ask him to tell us about his conversion. He is an old man now, and old men like to give reminiscences of their youth.' So they went to John, and found him at home. When he understood the object of their visit he said, 'Come in and sit down, and I will be delighted to tell you all about it,' and beginning with that night when for the first time he leaned his head on the bosom of his Master, he went on to tell how some of them

---

[1] Mr. Balfour-Melville, who has kindly supplied these notes, remembers that a banker sitting beside him at the time added up the sum as recorded and found this was correct.

had had their consciences awakened because of sin, and John the Baptist's preaching had deepened that feeling, but did not relieve it, till one day he said, 'Behold the Lamb of God that taketh away the sin of the world.' 'Then,' he said, 'two of us went to Him, and He was so gracious to us, and dealt with us so tenderly, that that night we gave ourselves to Him.' Then he told them of all that he had seen of Jesus till the close of His life, and of all his own experience since 'But,' said he, 'I have continued a sinner to the end, for when I was in Patmos, and was shown the great things that were shortly to come to pass, like a sinner I fell down to worship before the feet of the angel which showed me these things. I forgot he was but a servant,—a fellow-servant,—and that I must worship only God.'

From all parts of the world letters came to him asking for prayer, for counsel, for direction, and his opinion was regarded as final by many in all sections of the Church of God. Of the blessing received through his books he had grateful testimonies from time to time. Not long after the publication of the *Narrative of a Mission of Inquiry to the Jews*, a lady in England wrote telling him that it had been the means of the conversion of an infidel. Two of his smaller books—*The Gospel pointing to the Person of Christ*, a book for inquirers, and the *Brook Besor*, written for invalids—were very greatly blessed. A copy of another of his little books, *What gives Assurance*, was given by a gentleman to one who through serious illness had fallen into depression of mind. When visiting her husband, after the good woman's death, he told him that a great change had come to his wife after reading that book. 'She was just another woman, and she kept the precious little book in the "brods o' her Bible," and only parted once with it to a neighbour on

condition that it should be returned.' She passed away
in peace, repeating to herself shortly before the end,

> 'Safe in the arms of Jesus,
> Safe on His gentle breast !'

He had a singular gift of letter-writing. His letters
were generally very short, but in almost every one—even
in those about the most ordinary subjects—there is a
word or a thought which makes them valuable. For
example, he writes to one and another of his friends :—

'When you come to see us, come to help us by prayer, as well
as to drink water out of our well.'

'Come and spend a day or two here. We might perhaps be
mutually refreshed. Remember Emmaus.'

'Pray for blessing, for it is like the dew which Gideon prayed
for. It falls where it is sought.'

'Be thou in the fear of the Lord all the day long. Keep under
the light that beams from Jacob's ladder, and you will always have
a Bethel-fear.'

'Dwell in the Tabernacle under the Shadow of the Almighty,
and not a drop of wrath shall fall on a hair of your head. Walk,
too, in the light of the cloud of glory over the mercy-seat. It is
New Jerusalem glory.'

'Let us be like Jacob's sons ; go often to Joseph—our Joseph.
The corn of the Nile that overflows yearly is the best, and is the
likest to the corn of our God, proceeding as it does from His
overflowing and everflowing love.'

'Behold the fowls of the air ! how merrily they sing, not troubled
about next day's food or clothing. Be as they. Sing to your God
and Father merrily to-day, and let the morrow take thought for
itself.'

'What was the last nugget of gold of Ophir you found in reading the Word ? Do you not often say with one of your old friends,
the Fathers,

> "Adoro plenitudinem Scripturarum."'

'What of the gold-diggings ?' he writes again ; 'Any
recent discovery in the knowledge of Him who counsels

us to buy "gold tried in the fire"? Does not this mean such things as these, viz.

> 'Buy of me your ransom-money.
> 'Buy of me your golden harp.
> 'Buy of me the golden streets of the New Jerusalem.
> 'Buy back Paradise, for "the gold of that land is good."'

'I was greatly refreshed yesterday by two words from the mouth of the Lord in the verse, "For a small moment have I forsaken thee," etc. (Isa. liv. 7). The words are חֶסֶד עוֹלָם "the mercy *of an eternity!*' What is this that is coming to us, brother? *The mercy of a whole eternity!*'

'Notice Zech. ix. 13 : "I have filled the bow with Ephraim." When He uses you, He just makes you an arrow—fills His bow with you.'

'Follow the Shepherd, and remember, if you are following Him you will be sure to get a good mouthful of pasture every now and then. Our Shepherd would not lead us where nothing is to be found.'

'The "fragments" in the baskets, would not they keep for many days?'

One letter closes with the request, 'Sometimes think on us and ask something for us, for we are needy.' And another, 'This week is our Communion. *N.B.*—Remember in prayer a congregation in Glasgow needing rain from heaven.' Inside the envelope of a note addressed to one of his people is written : 'With the prayer, Eph. iii. 14–20, and the request, 1 Thess. v. 25. *N.B.*—Eph. vi. 18.' With a small subscription sent to a friend he wrote :—

'From an old disciple who remembers what the Master's blessing can do (John vi. 11). A barley loaf and a small fish from Scotland.'

'Prayer for saints and for those who "minister the gospel" is the oil which keeps bright all the weapons we use,—sword, shield,' etc.

'Study the fifteen prayers of Paul,' he wrote to one of his people, 'six in First and Second Thessalonians, two in Ephesians, two in Philippians, two in Colossians, two in Romans, one in Hebrews.

'Pray them too, and pray them often, and pray for me also.'

His letters help to explain how he was able to go on giving out to others from day to day so continually. His hand was always on the key of the storehouse of all grace, and his God was ever supplying all his need :—

'As to Saturday I have great, because conscientious, difficulties, because of my own soul which cannot stand three successive weeks of giving out, in Perth, Dundee, Edinburgh, and Kelso. Ah, brother, I am only longing to be so full that out of me shall flow rivers, ποταμοί —whole Niles or Rhines or Jordans—of living water. Happy day! and "yet a little while."'

'Vessels are not fountains. Vessels need to be filled as well as to give out to others.'

'Here is something to remember, Isa. xxvii. 3 : "I will water it every moment." When Alexander Somerville and I were in the Botanic Gardens we asked the superintendent about that passage. It is spoken of vines, and yet A. S. had in vain inquired in the East about it, for they all said that they did not water their vines. . . . "Well," the man said to me after a little thought, "I'll tell you what it may be. Notice the little tendrils of the vine. They have generally a drop at the end. This is to be accounted for by the fact that the vine has the power of condensing the vapour in the atmosphere around it, and so it keeps itself supplied with moisture." Is this not very instructive? God's vines are furnished with the capacity of drawing in moisture from around even when no shower falls (no sermon, no special ordinance), invisible as is the process to human eyes.' [1]

[1] This verse, 'I will water it every moment,' he called 'the Old Testament Eighth of Romans.'

The solemn sense of responsibility which he felt as a minister of the gospel is shown in his copy of Bridges' *Christian Ministry*, which he has marked and annotated till it has become almost a new book, in many ways descriptive of his own ministry. Nothing, however interesting, was allowed to interfere with the one great object of his life. In an address which he gave to the Finnieston Young Men's Literary Association in 1883 he told how some time before he had begun the study of Hebrew synonyms with the intention of perhaps writing a small book on the subject. He had made some progress in it, but stopped because he found it was interfering with his one great work. Even ordinary reading was not allowed to take up much of his time. If told of a very interesting book he would say, ' Lay it aside and I will read it in the holidays.' He watched himself with almost painful carefulness, and stirred others up to the same prayerful vigilance. One of his solemn sayings in regard to ministers was, ' The sins of teachers are the teachers of sins,' and he often quoted a remark about the Old Testament saints, ' Beware of the bad things of good men.'

' Let us stir one another up in the pursuit of holiness—fellowship with God. Samson's strength was only *indicated* by his long hair. It had a secret spring. Our success would not be our strength, nor would our enlarged preaching and diligent visiting ; yet these will begin to grow if we have access to the hidden source.'

' I am more than ever convinced that unholiness lies at the root of our little success. "*Holy* men of God spake to the fathers." It must be holy men still that speak with power. The only good thing I feel at present is the Word, and God there.'

' Write soon and tell me anything fitted to stir the

soul in sleepy days. . . . Do you ever feel that when there are no symptoms of converting work going on among your people, your own soul gets ungirt for work? I often find this, and I feel it at present. Even the wise virgins slumber.'

'Did you ever feel in preaching as if you were a blunt arrow? I felt so yesterday until about evening, when the Archer seemed to sharpen the point.'

Though unsparing of his own strength, he was always considerate of others. 'When your foot swells,' he used to say, 'the Lord does not want you to travel.'

During his summer holidays in 1890, he wrote to his Biblewoman, Miss Walker, cautioning her against overworking herself in his absence :—

'*Aros Cottage, Salen, Isle of Mull.*

'To the DEACONESS WALKER,
    who labours much in the Lord, greeting.

'Grace and peace be multiplied to you, day by day. A very old friend who lived in the land of Midian once gave a most needful and wise advise to a worker who was doing his best to shorten his valuable life. The worker's name was Moses, and the friend was Jethro. The people came to Moses "to inquire of God," and he was never done listening to them. "They stood by him from morning to evening." But wise and gracious Jethro saw it, and said, "*The thing that thou doest is not good*," and showed Moses how to "*make it easier for himself*": "so shalt thou be able to endure, and this people shall go to their place in peace," instead of letting him kill himself on their account! Is not that a good lesson for your study, that your mind may be perfectly at ease in taking *a long holiday*?

'The Pastor of the congregation sends this message to the Deaconess, thanking her for her blessed work in the past, but hoping that there is to be an hundredfold more to give thanks for in days coming.

'Meanwhile, pray for all the congregation and all the souls in the Mission District "without ceasing." And so, with the words of another old friend whom "the Spirit clothed" (1 Chron. xii. 18), this letter closes : "Peace, peace be unto thee, and peace be to thine helpers ; for thy God helpeth thee." Amen.

'Twenty-third day of the seventh month, 1890.'

'See that your last days are your best days,' were his words to believers, 'not like David, of some of whose descendants it was said in praise, "they walked in the *first* ways of their father David."' He seemed to have a solemn fear in his latter years lest he should "lose the things he had wrought," and not receive a full reward.

'We are not to indulge for a moment the belief : " Oh, I must count on a season of languor in my Christian life." Where did you find that in the Bible ? " Like the palm-tree flourishing," etc. Ask any gardener and he will tell you it is a sad indication of any plant to stop growing.'

'Our root is in Christ, and in the "love that passeth knowledge." We will grow up and flourish if our roots are in such a soil. If spared to old age, our fruit will be abundant. In our younger days a great deal is *blossom*, but as we grow older it is *fruit*. It does not make such an appearance, but it is more enduring.'

To others his earnestness and eager longing for the salvation of souls seemed to increase with his years. It was noticeable at the time of his ' Jubilee' (1888) how he exerted himself in every possible way, as if feeling that his days of work for the Master might soon be over.

'Plenty of work here now, and winter has come, but His yoke is "easy." Did you ever notice Christ says it is χρηστός, as if alluding to Χριστός.'

'It is constant work, but it is "vineyard" work, and work for the Master, who bore the burden and heat of the day.'

'We are alive, and many whom we started with have reached the goal. "In death there is no remembrance of Thee." Let us give thanks for life and work, even for care and weariness. "This is the fruit of my labour" —τοῦτό μοι καρπὸς ἔργου.'

'The night cometh, but thereafter the morning! the Resurrection-morning, when we shall know the results of present labour, and when we shall see Him as He is. . . It is a solemn thing to look back on so many years as I have had, and to look a little onward and see the Eternal Shore.'

'Oh, the memories of the past!' he wrote to an old friend. 'It needs the "Man that is the hiding-place" to keep them!'

Even when on his holidays, his people and his work occupied most of his thoughts. 'I am beginning to think of home and work in Finnieston,' he wrote to a lady in his congregation from his holiday retreat. 'I have been long away, but only I can work for you all at a distance in more ways than one.' From his summer quarters in Anwoth, he wrote one of his quaint and beautiful letters to two other members of his flock :—

'HONOURED SISTERS,—I am fain to reply to a question stated to me by a friend of yours and mine, who is here on a short sojourn. The question you have put is anent one passage of God's word, to wit, that in Matt. xviii. 10 where it is written, "Their angels do always behold the face of your Father." Ye say that a godly Professor of Divinity thinks that this teaches us "that angels, because of their charge over these little ones, have errands into the presence of their Father, and so have got a liberty to deal familiarly with Him (so to speak) which they would not have had but for the sake of the little ones." This is a blessed truth, I doubt not ; howbeit there is yet more honey to be found dropping from that wood of the Tree of Life, if only Jonathan's rod were dipt in the comb a second time. If we be spared to speak face to face, it will be pleasanter than to write about it with ink and paper, as the beloved John said on a like occasion to the "Elect Lady," as ye may read (2 John 12).

'But will you let me say yet more, for it is good that we as travellers to the same country stir up one another to quicken our pace. I know ye are not taking your Inn for your home, but are minding your inheritance in New Jerusalem. Ye need not marvel if every day some cross, less or more, be your portion. Till ye be in heaven, it will be but foul weather, one shower and then another. But if there were twenty crosses for this year written down for you in God's book of providence, they will soon be past ; ye will soon be at the nineteenth, and then there is but one more, and after that nothing ! for then ye shall lay your head on His bosom, and His own soft hand shall dry your face and wipe away your tears. Is this not true, worthy ladies, that it is a king's life to live upon the love of Christ ? I said this long ago to a worthy friend now in glory, and I think ye will say it was well spoken.

'My old mansion here, from which I used to go forth to my "walk" among the shady trees, has long since been taken down, and even so we also ourselves shall be ere long. But like the Sisters of Bethany, whom Jesus loved, your hearts' desire is to Him who is the Resurrection and the Life, who is coming soon to give us our house which is from heaven, which shall be eternal. He cannot come too soon.

'The minister of Christ who used to preach the word to your souls, and whom ye failed not to encourage many ways, intends to return home from his sojourn in these parts. In the end of this week he goes back with his household to the place of his ministry on the banks of the Clyde, though not so near your dwelling as formerly. You will not forget him, as he will not forget you. Pray for him, as I once said to Gordon of Garloch here, that in his work he may be "fraughted and full of Christ."

'Yours in His lovely and longed-for Jesus.'

Earthly honour had little attraction for him. The degree of Doctor of Divinity, conferred on him in 1873, gratified him as a token of regard from his own University of Edinburgh. To be asked to occupy the highest position in the Free Church as Moderator of her Assembly was a real cross to him, and made him write to Mr. Manson : 'It is a terrible dilemma I am placed in ; for letters come to me insisting that my responsibility will be something more than ordinary if I refuse —and yet I think, in accepting, the responsibility is no way less. Alas! how far down our Church has come when it asks such as me to take this office!'

His ambition was to 'know Christ,' and this one aim simplified his whole life. His obedience in the smallest details was very striking. It was not so much that he did not do wrong, but that he seemed always to do the things that pleased God. Those who lived with him cannot recall a single unworthy action in his life. Step by step he walked with God, doing everything as in His sight. 'You are not very holy if you are not very kind,' he used to say, and this spirit of love characterised his own actions. 'I have settled all—glad to be able to send out a cluster of grapes to moisten the parched lips of my brother,' he writes when sending some books to Mr. Milne in India. A favour shown to himself he regarded as shown to Christ in one of His members. For some friends who had given him the present of a Bible, he wrote in acknowledgment of their kindness :—

'AN INCIDENT, NEITHER CANONICAL NOR APOCRYPHAL, BUT TRUE.

'There were two sisters, related spiritually to Martha and Mary of Bethany, "whom Jesus loved," and who loved Jesus.

'Many years after the Master had gone away, and when many were beginning to talk about His coming back soon, these two sisters thought in their hearts that, meanwhile (since the Master was not here), they would like to show kindness to one of His disciples for His sake. They sent therefore sixty-six clusters of choice grapes, bound together in one.

'The disciple wondered, thanked them in his heart, prayed for rich returns of blessing on Martha and Mary, and sent back this request :

'My dear sisters, will you help me to press the grapes into the cup which I shall try to hand to you from week to week, when we meet to taste the New Wine of the Kingdom?' Eph. iii. 14-21.

To another member of his church he wrote a very

characteristic note of thanks for a present received from her :—

'*Decr.* 15*th*, 1885.

'A grateful Pastor, whose great-grandfather had charge of the Sheep in Fetlar and Yell, Shetland Isles, sends thanks to the Sheep who has so kindly presented him with Shetland wool, so soft and warm!

'Great Shepherd of the Sheep, bless this member of Thy flock with a new blessing and a fuller!'

Burdened as he must have been with the care of others, his calmness and freedom from worry were very remarkable, as well as his happy and ever-thankful spirit. 'We should be always wearing the garment of praise, not just waving a palm-branch now and then.'

'Thanksgiving is the very air of heaven.'

'There is one ear that listens to every note of praise from every one of His people. Never say, "*I* need not praise Him. He will not miss *me* out of the choir." "Bless the Lord, O *my* soul."'

'Why should we be afraid to rejoice, when God is not afraid to trust us with joy?'

'Jacob said, "I shall go down to the grave with sorrow." What a mistake! He went down singing!'

'"All joy and peace in believing." "*All* joy," complete joy, that will fill every crevice of your vacant heart. "*All* peace," that will not allow room for a single fear.'

'The oil of joy calms down the waves of trouble.'

'God's people,' he said, 'sometimes take fits of sea-sickness in sailing to Immanuel's Land. They give way to hard thoughts of God.' He asked some friends on whom he was calling how they were getting on. They said, 'Not very well; we are not getting the rich food for our souls we used to get. We were just saying we are getting husks now.' 'Oh, I see,' was his reply.

'You've been having a grumble-meeting! Did you ever notice when we grumble to one another we grow discontented and bitter, and that is grieving to the Holy Spirit? But, when we go and tell the Lord, it has a very different effect. We get tenderness and sympathy.'

Speaking one day of the conversion of the Philippian jailer, he said, 'Oh, brethren, I see it now! They had spread the Gospel over the whole city by their *prayers* and *praises*, and they thought it was to be by their *preaching*!'

'A gloomy believer,' he said, 'is surely an anomaly in Christ's kingdom'; and gloominess was the last thing to be associated with him. An indescribable sweetness and mellowness characterised his old age, and robbed it of all sadness. Left alone, the last of a family of eleven brothers and sisters, his old friends nearly all gone from him, his joy in Christ triumphed over every sorrow.

'Garments fresh, and feet unweary,
Told how God had brought him through.'

'This season,' he wrote in October 1882, 'has been sending me back to eighteen years ago—a never-to-be-forgotten time (his wife's death). I thought then that life could never again be lightsome, but I find that the more of Christ we enjoy, the more we are able to bear.'

'When we have truly found Christ, we can go through the world alone.'

'If you are a child of God, there is nothing in the world you cannot do without, and have a heaven in the want of it.'

When the last of his brothers was taken away, and he alone was left behind, he stood beside his grave—the only mourner with a smile on his face. As the earth was heaped on the coffin he turned to a friend beside him and said, 'I know that he shall rise again!' More

than once, referring to his age he said, ' I don't feel that
I am an old man, but I know I must be, for Barzillai was
fourscore years old, and the Bible says he was " a *very
aged man* ! " ' His friend Major Whittle asked him one
day if he had found it harder to be a Christian as an old
man than as a young man. Dr. Bonar turned his sunny
face towards him and said, ' Oh, I don't think anything
about growing old. I just keep on, doing each day's
work by itself, and looking to the Lord for daily grace.
I don't feel old. I feel just as young as I ever did.'

His last summer holiday, in 1892, was spent at Brae-
field, Portpatrick, and the pleasant walks and rambles
there will ever be a sunny memory to his friends. He
preached in the Free Church during his stay, and took
a great interest in the open-air meetings begun on
Sabbath afternoons by his son-in-law, Mr. Oatts. On
the last Sabbath of August he conducted the meeting
himself, and as he was walking home a stranger came
up to him and asked if he might speak to him. He
said he had been for thirty-seven years in America, and
was home for a holiday, had read all his books, but had
never expected to see himself. When returning to
Glasgow a few days later Dr. Bonar stopped at Stran-
raer and visited an aged friend, Mrs. Cunningham, at
North-west Castle. ' When I met him at the railway
station,' writes her son, the Rev. J. G. Cunningham, ' he
told me that he must call for his old friend the Rev.
George Sherwood, and he carried out his purpose, play-
fully disregarding the remonstrances of his family
against the additional fatigue. I accompanied him, and
was struck with the swift pace which he easily maintained. On our way I was accosted by an ostler
belonging to one of the hotels, who asked me with
respectful interest to tell him the name of the old
minister who was with me, " for," said he, " I saw him at

the Port, preaching in the open air, and I was glad to hear him." Dr. Bonar shook hands warmly with his grateful hearer, to whom that sermon had given a real and unlooked-for pleasure. The interview between my dear mother and Dr. Bonar was truly affecting. They knew well that it was their last meeting on earth; and they spoke with calm and grateful hearts of the "goodness and mercy" which had followed them for more than fourscore years of pilgrimage, and of their hope of welcome at no distant date into "the house of the Lord for ever." Within a few months both of the venerable pilgrims met again "in that better country into which no enemy ever entered, and from which no friend ever went away." '

The failure of his strength was very gradual, and not very perceptible except to those around him. His handwriting grew less firm, and his memory began to fail him in little things. One day, not very long before his death, a gentleman met him in Howard Street, and found that he was quite confused as to where he was. He kindly put him on the right way, and as they parted Dr. Bonar thanked him and said, 'I've just been thinking that I have been like Peter when the angel took him out of prison. Poor man, he did not know where he was!'

On the 31st of October 1892, writing to a friend about the sudden death of Mr. Inglis of Dundee, he says: 'What a surprise to find himself all at once among those who "do immediately pass into glory." . . . May we be "found of Him in peace," like our brother, when our evening comes.'

The post had sounded his horn at his chamber-door, and from the Celestial City had come the message: 'Thy Master has need of thee, and in a very little time thou must behold His face in brightness.' His last days were spent in the same unceasing ministry for others that had been the joy of his life, and, as he lay on his dying bed, it was to his work that his thoughts were ever turning.

After only two days of illness, he passed away on Friday, the 30th of December 1892.

'When I think of dying,' he once said, 'I think of it something in this way. I fancy myself going home from a meeting some night, and I feel not very well. I get worse, then I become unconscious, and then I know nothing more until I am in the presence of a Throne. There are seats around the Throne, and I am pointed to one which is vacant. I am told that it is for me. Then I see a Hand, and when I look at it I see it is a pierced Hand, and it holds a crown over my head! But, oh! the weight of glory is so great I cannot bear it, and so I lift it off, and cast it at the foot of the Throne, saying, "*Thou* art worthy; for Thou wast slain, and hast redeemed us to God by Thy blood!"'

FAITH AND DOCTRINE

'Then said Greatheart to Mr. Valiant-for-truth, "Thou hast worthily behaved thyself. Let me see thy sword." So he showed it to him. When he had taken it in his hand and looked thereon a while, he said, "Ha! it is a right Jerusalem blade."

'*Val.* "It is so. Let a man have one of these blades, with a hand to wield it, and skill to use it, and he may venture upon an angel with it. He need not fear its holding, if he can but tell how to lay on. Its edges will never blunt. It will cut flesh and bones, and soul, and spirit, and all."'—*John Bunyan.*

CHAPTER IX

' LORD, never let any one occupy this pulpit who does not preach Christ and Him crucified,' was Dr. Bonar's prayer one day in his own church; and his oft-repeated desire for himself was that he might never to the day of his death preach to his people, or be with them in any of their meetings, without saying something about what gives peace to the sinner. Once, after preaching in St. Peter's, Dundee, upon the text, ' Thine eyes shall see the King in His beauty,' Mr. M'Cheyne said to him as they walked home together, ' Brother, I enjoyed your sermon; to me it was sweet. You and I and many, I trust, in our congregations shall see the King in His beauty. But, my brother, you forgot there might be many listening to you to-night, who, unless they are changed by the grace of God, shall never see Him in His beauty.'

Whether as the effect of this kindly reproof or not, certain it is that Dr. Bonar never afterwards preached a sermon in which he did not commend Christ to the unsaved, and rarely, if ever, closed without urging on his hearers the immediate acceptance of the Saviour. ' A sinner,' he often repeated, ' so long as he is un-pardoned, has a right to only one thing in the universe —only one—and that is the blood of the Lord Jesus Christ.'

The atoning sacrifice of the Son of God formed the

133

central point of all his preaching.   The Cross was 'the
breaking of God's alabaster-box, the fragrance of which
has filled heaven and earth.'   This little world was 'the
altar of the universe on which lay the Almighty Sacrifice.   The Incarnation was but the scaffolding for the
Atonement.   It is the Cross that shows us the love of
God at a white heat.   The earliest form of worship
was the lamb slain : Behold Abel's altar !   The latest
form of worship is the Lamb slain who is now on the
throne of the universe.'   Round the Cross he gathered
the whole Word of God, and all the dim foreshadow-
ings of type and prophecy met in Him who died on
Calvary.   The infinite fulness of this Sacrifice—'a whole
Christ between the humblest sinner and the smallest
drop of God s wrath '—God's only-begotten Son, 'the
half of His own joy given up for a time for us '—was
what he rejoiced to proclaim.   To many his preaching
of Jesus Christ as the living personal Saviour was a
revelation and the beginning of a new life.   This
Saviour and His atoning work stands between the
coming sinner and every dark and difficult doctrine.
Longings for pardon, for rest, for peace are met by the
simple acceptance of this Saviour, whose blood speaks
peace to the conscience and whose love brings rest to
the heart.[1]   So powerful is this sprinkled blood that it
can carry a sinner into the holiest of all to hold communion at the Mercy-seat with a reconciled God and
Father.   'One touch of this cleansing blood seals the
soul for service.'   Its voice—like the sound of the waves
on the shore—is ever speaking peace in a believer's ear,
'sometimes loudly, sometimes less clearly, but always
speaking.'   'If a believer can do without the blood he is
a backslider.'   'At the Bush Moses was forbidden to draw

---

[1] He used sometimes to quote, with warm approval, the saying of a
devoted Methodist minister, '*Live in the* Sacrifice !   *Live in the* Sacrifice.'

nigh, but afterwards on the Mount he went up into the very presence of God. What made the difference? At the Bush *there was no sacrifice.'* [1]

Once when asked by Mr. Moody to tell the young ministers gathered at Northfield the secret of a consecrated life, his simple answer was, ' I can only say to my young brethren that for forty years there has not been a day that I have not had access to the Mercy-seat.'

When saying good-bye to some friends in whose house he had been staying, one of them said to him, 'Dr. Bonar, you are like the palm-tree flourishing in the courts of the Lord.' He turned round, and, laying his hand on his friend's shoulder, he said eagerly, 'And if we are planted in the House of the Lord, then you know where our roots will be? *Under the altar.'*

The Person and work of the Lord Jesus Christ occupied him at all times. When holding Him up before any who were seeking salvation, he used to say :

'Salvation is not fleeing to the shadow of the great Rock, but it is fleeing to the Man who is a Hiding-place, and laying our head on His bosom.'

'Many want salvation, but they do not want the Saviour.'

'The work of Christ is the open door for the sinner, but Christ Himself stands behind it waiting to welcome him.'

An invalid lady in the country sent him a message that she had not enough of joy. He sent back the answer, ' Tell Mrs. C. it is not more *joy* she needs, but more of *Christ.'*

A Christian Jew who had brought another to church with him met Dr. Bonar as he came out, and told him

---

[1] When reading at family worship the narrative of God's rebuke and Israel's repentance in Judges ii. 1-5, he said before closing the book : ' Sorrow can never put away sin, sacrifice alone can do that ; so they not only wept at Bochim, but "they sacrificed there unto the Lord."

about the young man's difficulties. 'He won't receive Christ.' 'Ah,' said Dr. Bonar, 'that's because you don't know Him. All who know Him receive Him.'

'Draughts of the water of life are just fresh views of Christ. The promises are streams coming down from Christ's heart.'

'Peace is the mantle dropped by Christ.' 'The invitation, "Come unto Me," is like the waving of the fringe of His robe as He moves along by the shores of the Sea of Galilee.' Christ's life of obedience was 'a walk from Bethlehem to Calvary without a stumble.' His righteousness was 'the robe in which He walked through our world every day, and which, when He had finished His walk,—as Elijah left his mantle to Elisha,— He left for us to wear.' To get a deeper sense of sin is to look at the price paid for our pardon.'

'If ever there was anything that, more terribly than hell itself, showed the sinfulness of sin, it was the Saviour's agony in the Garden.'

'When we count the pieces of the Ransom-money, may we see what a terrible evil sin is.'

'It is not a sight of our sinful heart that humbles us, it is a sight of Jesus Christ: I am undone, *because mine eyes have seen the King.*'

'If deep sorrow and remorse could blot out sin, hell would be a great Calvary.' 'There is nothing Satan fears so much as the blood of Christ.' 'Purity of heart (Psalm xxvi. 6) depends upon the place we are giving in our consciences to the blood of Christ.'

'Power over habits of sin may be gained by confessing sin.' 'He breaks the power of cancelled sin.' We can also say, 'He breaks the power of sin confessed.' 'No man ever honestly confesses before God the sin he has done till that sin is taken away. It is a full pardon that makes a man guileless.'

Of one who dwelt very much upon sin, without, as he thought, dwelling sufficiently on the power of the blood to cleanse, he said, ' I think his gospel is the miry clay.'

'We are called "more than conquerors" not at the end of our course, but while it is going on.'

'You need not be afraid of too much grace. Great grace never makes a man proud. A little grace is very apt to make a man be puffed up.'

'Sin is not simply going against our conscience ; it is going against the law, though conscience keep silence.'

Some one told him that for six months she had not consciously committed any sin. 'And are you not very proud of it?' said Dr. Bonar. 'Yes,' she replied, 'I am!'

'Faith grows upon the soil of felt sin.' 'Great faith is simple faith. If you are seeking great faith, remember the simpler it is the greater it will be.'

'There was a defect in the faith of many who came to Christ to be healed. But it was not the strength of their faith Christ looked to, but the reality of it. They got the cure, though the hand that touched Him trembled.'

' " My " is the handle of faith.'

He made frequent use of four lines of a hymn written by his brother :—

> 'Upon a life I did not live,
> Upon a death I did not die ;
> Another's life, another's death,
> I stake my whole eternity.'

'When I write a hymn,' he says in a letter to one of his children, ' I think it will begin

> "*Looking always to Jesus.*"

'I am not sure of the way some people sing "There is life for a look." It must be a *steady* look.'

To one seeking full assurance he wrote :—

'Just as the bitten Israelites were healed every time they felt the bite of the fiery serpents, simply by looking to the Brazen Serpent, so we, every time we feel our soul dark, or sad, or unbelieving, are directed to fix our thoughts *at once* on Christ, the Lamb of God and the Priest. "Look unto Me and be saved" (Isa. xlv. 22). "They looked unto Him and were lightened" (Psalm xxxiv. 5). "Therefore I will look to the Lord" (Micah vii. 7). "Run the race looking (not at your own feet, or thinking of your own running but) *unto Jesus*" (Heb. xii. 2). Compare this with God looking on us, and on what we look to. "The bow shall be in the cloud, *and I will look upon it,* and remember the Covenant" (Gen. ix. 16). "When *I see* the blood I will pass over you" (Exod. xii. 13). *We* look on the blood of Atonement, and God looks on *us* well pleased when we are so employed. Do you sometimes sit down and sing to yourself such a hymn as—

> "Walk in the light, so shalt thou know," etc.
> "I heard the voice of Jesus say," ' etc.

'Doubts and fears are not marks of God's children. They are remnants of the old nature—specks upon the eye of faith. You should give them no quarter.'

'If you say it is good to have doubts, you are just saying, "I will not take all that God offers." Faith takes a whole Christ for itself: "My Lord and my God."'

One who had not assurance he described as believing in Christ, but not believing what He says. 'Faith dwells at Jerusalem. Full assurance goes into the palace and sees the King's face.' 'It is the privilege and the duty of believers (looking at the blood) not to have a fear or a doubt. You can't honour God more, you can't please the Holy Spirit more, or Christ more, than by putting unbounded confidence in the blood.'

'Would it have been right,' he asked, 'for the prodigal to sit at the table dropping tears into his cup, saying, "I can't be glad," when the Father said "It is meet that we should make merry and be glad?"'

'John did not rise from the Table because there was a doubt about himself and his steadfastness. He leaned all the harder [ἀνέπεσεν] on his Master's bosom.'

His adherence to the old truths never wavered, nor his simple unquestioning faith in the Word of God as his guide. Some of his last sermons were preached upon subjects in the Epistle of Jude, which many shrink from as unpleasant and unpopular. Sin and its punishment—eternal banishment from God's presence—were part of the 'whole counsel of God' which he must declare. 'To fall into the hands of the living God—to be crushed between the millstones of omnipotence.' 'Jesus spoke these terrible words about hell in the eighteenth of Matthew, with a little child in his arms.' 'No one preached more about hell than Christ did. You remember His thrilling narrative of the rich man and Lazarus; as if He would pursue the sinner with a flaming sword until he entered the city of refuge. But "they will not believe"—although Lazarus was the preacher, and his text, "Not a drop of water to cool the tongue."'

'I think He will weep over the lost as He did over Jerusalem. It will be something to be said for ever in heaven, "Jesus wept as He said, Depart, ye cursed." But then it was absolutely necessary to say it.'

'I think that the shower of fire and brimstone was wet with the tears of God as it fell, for God has "no pleasure in the death of him that dieth."'

A lady whom he was asked to visit during an illness said to him, 'I've been trying for some days with all my might to believe in annihilation; but I can't.' 'I can tell you something better,' said Dr. Bonar. 'If you believe in Christ your *sin* will be annihilated.'

Divine sovereignty was a subject he often referred to in his preaching, but never as an impassable barrier between God and a sinner.

'You will never get light by looking into darkness. Paul does not plunge into the depths and drown himself. He stands on the shore and adores: "O the depths!"' etc. (Romans xi. 33).

'"Strong meat" is not what are called the "deep doctrines" of Scripture. "Strong meat" is really what you had last Sabbath at the Communion-table—"the finest of the wheat."'

'Doctrine and hearing of the Word abound,' he wrote after a visit to the North, 'though the doctrine is not what we in the South reckon to be the very truth, for sovereignty is thrust in at all points as if to overawe the sinner, and make him draw back from touching even the hem of the garment. They say that they do it to empty and humble the sinner. Oh for showers of the Spirit! for, when the Spirit comes, all things take their proper place.'

'Take care,' he used to say, 'that you never mix anything with the "finest of the wheat."' Referring to the doctrine of election he said, 'If God were to reveal your election to you, you would believe in yourself instead of in Christ.' At another time, speaking of the same subject, he made the striking remark, 'We have often found that Satan takes the substantial food, which God has provided for His own children, to poison sinners with.' One of his quaint sayings, in stirring believers up to more watchfulness, was: 'If Satan was dangerous when Paul wrote his epistles, how much more dangerous must he be now, for he has got so much more experience?'

Some one remarked in his hearing that she did not like doctrine; it was not practical. At once he replied, 'Doctrine *is* practical, for it is that that stirs up the heart.'

The work of the Holy Spirit was a special feature of his preaching, and the love of that Spirit as revealed in His written Word. 'Every line in this inspired Bible is wet with the dew of the Spirit's love.'

'"The sword of the Spirit"—the sword which the Spirit uses. The sword is made up of various parts: the long blade, the handle, etc. And so the Scriptures have many parts, but the Gospel is the sharp point by which it pierces the soul.'

The Word of God, from Genesis to Revelation, was the food by which his soul was nourished, and the weapon by which he fought his battles and gained his victories. So readily did a scriptural phrase or a scriptural illustration drop from his lips, that it almost seemed as if he thought in scriptural language. As he was walking home from church one evening, his daughter offered to carry his umbrella for him. He declined to give it to her, and said to a friend who was with them, 'We always like to have something in our hand when we are walking. I have noticed that. I wonder if we shall have the same feeling hereafter, for, do you notice, they carry "palms in their hands"?'

On the morning of the last day of his life, a friend called just as he was having a poultice administered. He looked up brightly, saying, 'I am just like Hezekiah: I am getting on a plaster!'

A meeting of special interest had been held from which one of his daughters had been unavoidably absent. As soon as he returned from it, he said to her, thinking of her disappointment, 'Remember there were two angels absent from the Ascension!'

A friend once referred at a meeting to his originality in finding subjects for sermons and addresses, and said, 'I don't know where Dr. Bonar gets all his texts.' Dr. Bonar lifted his Bible and quietly held it out to him.

His prayer one morning was, 'Make Thy Word a candle to reveal sin, and a leaf from the Tree of Life to heal.' In public reading of the Scriptures, no portion was ever passed over because of its difficulty or ob-

scurity, but every word and phrase were explained with
care and minuteness. An exposition of the first eight
chapters of 1 Chronicles[1] was given with the preface:
'This is God calling the roll of mankind;' and what at
first had seemed a record of unmeaning and forgotten
names, became a history of men and women, with hopes,
and fears, and aspirations like those of a present time.

As he read the fifth chapter of Genesis, with its melan-
choly refrain,—'and he died, and he died,'—he came to
the twenty-fourth verse, 'Enoch walked with God : and
was not ; for God took him.' He stopped and said, 'A
triumphal arch amid the tombs!'

Another remark of his on the same subject was:
Enoch walked with God, and one day he took a very
long walk, for he never came back again!'

When describing a scriptural incident he sometimes
gave full play to his imagination, and, with a graphic
touch here and there, brought the whole scene vividly
before the eye, as for example, when he described the
poor woman of 'the wives of the sons of the prophets'
(2 Kings iv.) following Elisha's instructions, and sending
her sons to borrow empty vessels from her neighbours.
'Reuben, you go up the street, and Samuel, you go
down the street, and ask all the neighbours for the
loan of empty vessels.' 'But what will they say to us,
mother?' 'They will say nothing, but give you the
dishes!'

Sometimes his quaint use of a scriptural illustration
had a happy effect in restoring harmony or carrying
a point. A well-known instance of this was his reference to the students in his closing address as Moderator
of the Free Church Assembly in 1878. 'We need not
be very much surprised,' he said, 'that those young

[1] He contributed 'Readings in 1 Chronicles' to the *Quarterly Journal
of Prophecy*, from 1857 to 1861.

"sons of the prophets" are rather prone to question the positive conclusions of older men. This was the tendency of the "sons of the prophets" even in the days of Elisha. There were schools, if not colleges, at Bethel and at Jericho : and you may remember how the youthful disciples there, not satisfied in regard to Elijah's translation, insisted that fifty of the most gifted of their number should go and search hill and valley for themselves. Again and again did the prophet assure them that it would prove only a waste of time and labour ; and when at length he yielded, and they went forth with all the confidence of youth, how did it end ? They came back to report that the old prophet was right after all. No doubt he smiled with mild satisfaction as he reminded them, " Did I not say unto you, Go not!"'

A friend one day asked him what he thought about the young man mentioned in Mark xiv. 51. 'I have a fable about him,' he said. 'He heard the singing in the Upper Room—the Lord was leading it—He raised the tune, and then the fishermen joined in it so heartily that the young man stopped to listen. Then he watched them as they went out, and followed them over the brook Kedron, and was lying among the olives to see what would happen when the band of soldiers came.'[1]

Some friends were talking with him about the fact that a stranger is very often used for the conversion of one whose parents and friends have prayed and watched over him. Dr. Bonar said, 'Now, give me a scriptural illustration of that.' No one did, so he said, 'Timothy, "*my own son in the faith.*" The child of Eunice and Lois! I daresay Eunice was greatly

---

[1] 'Bonar's fables' were what some of his friends called his speculations on Bible incidents. Mr. Moody used to say, 'Now, I want to hear some more fables!'

disappointed that it was not she, after all, that was used.   It was an itinerant evangelist!'

Speaking of Eutychus (Acts xx. 9) he said, 'It's not fair of Dr. Watts to make Eutychus a warning to sleepy hearers.   He's a warning to beadles to ventilate the church properly!'

As authority for beginning public worship with the singing of a psalm, he quoted Elisha's example in 2 Kings iii., when he asked for a minstrel to play, and the camp was calmed and solemnised.

To a friend he remarked about 1 Cor. xvi. 12: 'What a comfort that verse is!   People sometimes write so pressingly : "You must come, it is an opportunity of usefulness."   Paul says Apollos would not come, and he is not blamed for it.'

'Did you ever notice, in Acts xvi. 6, 7, how the Holy Ghost guides the heralds of salvation to their proper sphere?   On two occasions the Holy Spirit hindered Paul from going to places he wished to visit —Asia and Bithynia.   He was (so to speak) candidate for these two places, but the seven churches of Asia were reserved for John's ministry, and Bithynia (1 Pet. i. 1) for Peter's.   Paul must go away to Macedonia.'

'Why did Thomas not go to the meeting that night with the other disciples ?   I think he said, "What is the use of going ?   *The Master* won't be there!"'

Upon 1 Sam. iii. 4 he remarked, 'I think God spoke in Eli's voice so as not to frighten Samuel.'   Peter he described (Matt. xvi. 22) as 'the New Testament Uzzah trying to hold up the Ark.'

His commentary on Dan. vi. 18, 19, was 'Never put your name to a paper you have not read!'

A favourite fancy of his was, that the star in the East was the old Pillar-cloud.

He used to say that he thought the beggar at

the Beautiful Gate of the Temple had been a careless and unbelieving man, or he might have been healed long before; for we read, in Matt. xxi. 14, 'that on a certain day the blind and the lame came to Christ in the Temple and " He healed them." '

'It is a very striking thing that there is not an instance of any one in the New Testament bringing a gift to Christ when he came to be healed. Yet in the Old Testament we see this was a common custom.'

'Paul had to escape in a basket! the man God wrought such wonderful things by, had to escape in a most commonplace way. I daresay some people would like that Elijah had been fed by eagles rather than by ravens; but that is not God's way. He delivers believers in a common way.'

'Where did the ravens get the flesh they carried to Elijah? I think they picked it off Baal's altars !'

He liked to talk about angels and their work for us, and used to say he had not one guardian angel but hundreds.

'Why did the angel tell Peter in the prison to rise up "quickly"? Because he knew that, if he did not rise at once, he would go to sleep again! Even angels never lose time. They have plenty of work to do for the Lord.'

'Angels will never be kings. They will always be servants.'

'It is a good thing angels were not sent to preach to us. I would go far to hear an angel preach, but I don't think I would get much good from his sermon. I would come away thinking of his beautiful words and his persuasive tongue, but perhaps saying, "It is all very well for that angel to talk about the miry clay, but he does not know how stiff it is ! He never was in it." '

'"The tongue of angels" is the only bit of his experience in the Third Heavens that Paul gives us. He seems to have heard angels speak, or perhaps sing. Paul was a man of extraordinary grace to be contented to be so long upon earth after being in the Third Heavens, and not to pine to be back. He heard "unspeakable words" there. I think he must have heard the Saviour's voice speaking to His redeemed ones.'

'Reading the Gospels,' he said, 'is like walking in Galilee. There is nothing I enjoy more.'

He talked of the men and women of the Bible as of his familiar friends, and could not bear a suggestion of the Old Testament saints being on a lower platform than those of later times.

'We shall sit down *with* Abraham, Isaac, and Jacob in the kingdom—not *above* them—for they hoped in God while still in the shadows.'

'Elijah had such fellowship with God that he could say, "The Lord before whom I stand." Gabriel could not say more than that when he came down in after-days.'

'Did you ever notice that when the Jews said that Stephen blasphemed Moses, the Lord put upon him the same glory that He put upon Moses, and his face shone?'

In reference to the indwelling of the Holy Spirit, he said, 'There was the same well of water in the soul of the Old Testament saint as in the New Testament saint, but the water in that well never rose very high except in a few cases. We may say the well was just half-full in Old Testament times. But when Christ had finished His work, when "Jesus was glorified," then the rivers poured out of the well, because the waters poured in so abundantly. There never were two ways of saving souls. Always by union to Christ through the indwelling of the Spirit.'

'God fed His church on crumbs at first,' he used to say. 'Enoch lived on two crumbs of the bread of life, for all revealed Scripture then was "the seed of the woman," etc., and " Behold, the Lord cometh ! " etc. But what a life he led on these two crumbs ! And Noah in the Ark with no more. How that man stood out against a whole world ! O brethren, how the crumbs of the Bread of Life feed!' 'Caleb lived very much on one promise for forty years.'

When visiting his people he used to ask, 'Do you read regularly through the sixty-six books of the Bible, and not trust to little text-books?' 'Have you got a letter from the King to-day?' was a favourite question, when he wanted to introduce a conversation on that morning's portion of the Scripture.

Some friends who were studying the Book of Ezekiel told him they did not understand it very well. He said, 'I am glad you are reading Ezekiel's book before you meet him. What would he say if you met him in heaven and told him you had never read his book?'[1]

Often he used to say, 'Notice the *little* things in the Bible.' One morning, at the weekly meeting in his study, when the Bible-woman and missionary met with him for prayer, Miss Walker gave as her text for the day, 1 Cor. xv. 58, 'Be ye steadfast, unmoveable,' etc., 'forasmuch as ye know that your labour shall not be in vain in the Lord.' 'Stop!' said Dr. Bonar, 'is it " *shall be* " in your Bible? Look again. "Forasmuch as ye know that your labour *is* not in vain in the Lord."'

He strongly insisted that a text must not be taken

---

[1] He more than once took this way of impressing on others the import-ance of reading the Old Testament, and the impossibility of understanding the New Testament without the Old.

out of its connection to suit our purposes. 'Once,' he said, ' I was visiting a young man dying of consumption, and one day I found both his wife and himself much brighter than before. They said they had got a text which had encouraged them greatly. It was, " I shall not die but live," etc. They had no right to the text, and the young man died soon after.'

The whole Bible was to him bright with the promise of the Lord's Return, and this expectation gave joy and hopefulness to his whole life. Sorrow and bereavement made him think of the glorious time when 'death shall have become resurrection ;' pain and suffering reminded him of the 'new heavens and the new earth' yet to come. 'You will soon be a king. Why not think of your kingdom ?' he writes to a friend. 'Are you content with the Lord's gracious letter to you when you might rather be wearying for Himself ? I know that "this same Jesus" is as precious to you as to any of us, but when will you be a " man of Galilee," gazing up into heaven ?' To another friend he writes : 'Are you loving Christ's appearing and His kingdom ? If not, He hath somewhat against thee.'

'Many people nowadays,' he said, 'miss out the first part of the verse : "the grace of God which bringeth salvation," and go on to talk of the next part : "denying ungodliness and worldly lusts," etc. You say "that's dreadful !" Yes, but I know some Christians who miss out the last clause altogether : "looking for that blessed hope !"'

'Some Christians make a great mistake. They think that because Christ said it was expedient that He should go away, therefore it is expedient that He should *stay* away! He went away to present His finished work to the Father, but He must come back again.'

'I find the thought of Christ's Coming,' he said, 'very helpful in keeping me awake. Those who are waiting for His appearing will get a special blessing. Perhaps they will get nearer His Person. I sometimes hope it will be so, and that He will beckon me nearer to Him if I am waiting for Him ; just as at a meeting, you often see one beckoned to come up to the platform nearer the speakers.'

At a meeting in Philadelphia in 1881, to bid him farewell, the chairman—the late George Stewart—closed his address by saying that 'the Lord, the Righteous Judge, would give to His dear servant a crown of righteousness at the great day.' He sat down, and, on rising to reply, Dr. Bonar said, '"*And not to me only, but to all them also that love His appearing.*"'

As his ministry drew near its close, he often said to his people, '*I* may not live to see Him return, but I expect some of you listening to me will.' And to a friend he wrote : ' Christ's Coming is nearer and nearer. "When He cometh (we may say in another sense than the woman of Samaria, and yet like her) *He will tell us all things.*"' His Prophetic Lectures, delivered once a month on Sabbath evenings, from 1879 to 1883, will long be remembered. He had great enjoyment in them himself, and his voice, which even then was often feeble, seemed to regain its power as it proclaimed, through the crowded church, the Coming of the King of Glory. He very seldom spoke of his own death, though his diary shows how often it was in his thoughts.

When referring at his weekly prayer-meeting to the death of Dr. Somerville, who that morning had passed away, he spoke of what is called ' preparation for death,' and of 'dying grace.' 'I doubt,' he said, 'if there is such a thing, more than just the grace we need to live every day. Comparatively few of God's people have triumphant deaths. You are not triumphant when you fall asleep, and that's what death is,—falling asleep. We should be living so that we could be ready any day to go. If you were to go to call on some Christian friend, and the servant were to tell you at the door, "Oh, he's gone!" Would you feel you almost *envy* him? Are you living so that the only difference in your life really that death would make—if you were told "an hour later and you will be gone"—would be to make you say, "Well, my fellowship with the Lord will be *closer* then, but I've had fellowship with Him all day." When Elijah was told he was to be taken up, he went on doing his ordinary work, visiting the schools of the prophets. The only difference in his action was, that he wanted Elisha to leave him, that he might spare him the pain of the separation. But he did not spend the day in prayer or in any special *preparation*, as we call it. What we need for death is just what we need every day : the Saviour Himself with us.'

'We have boldness to enter into the holiest by the blood of Jesus. What more do we need in going into His presence?'

'"The *dead in Christ* shall rise first." A beautiful expression. It always reminds me of a mother with her dead infant lying on her bosom. Christ has His dead lying on His bosom, waiting for the resurrection.'

'The man who sees Christ in life is sure to see Him in the valley of the shadow of death.'

One who had always had a fear of death told him on her dying bed, that she had completely lost it by fixing her thoughts on that passage, 'I have the keys of hell and of death.' She thought, 'If Jesus has the keys of death, then the first face I shall see will be His!'

'Rest—glory—Christ. I think these three words,' he said, 'tell all that we know of the intermediate state. The Holy Spirit always hastens us on to the resurrection.'

'The intermediate state is Heaven's Upper Room, where the Master is, and where He will say unutterable things.'

'Elijah would get a welcome when he went up, but what work he got, we can't tell. We do not know what work disembodied spirits get to do. Down here we are just at school, and in the lowest class too. But we shall have our grand work afterwards.'

He sometimes used a familiar illustration to describe the intermediate state after death. 'There are the two classes: the ungodly and the godly. A man who has committed a crime is arrested and put in prison. Although judgment has not been passed upon him, he is securely locked up, and deprived of all his liberties. The terrible thought, that he must appear before the Judge and hear His final sentence, is always before him. The state of the godly, on the other hand, may be illustrated thus. A rich friend invites you to dine with him. On the appointed day you go to his house, and are shown into the drawing-room, where the guests are received by the host. The time until all the invited guests have arrived is passed in meeting friends, and in the presence and society of the host. When all have assembled, a bell sounds, and the whole company pass into the dining-hall where the feast is spread. So it will be at the great Supper of the Lamb.'

'Live for the Lord to-day, and look for His Coming to-morrow' was a rule he impressed on others, and carried out in his own life. The love of Christ constrained him to service beyond that of most men, and made that service a delight. Preaching was a necessity of his life. He never grew tired of it, and sometimes, indeed, found it difficult to get as much as he wanted. When one of his elders remonstrated with him for preaching too often during his holidays, he replied :—

> ''Tis joy, not duty,
> To speak His beauty !'

'I long,' he says at another time, 'to speak to the troubled soul about Jesus the Peace-maker, saying to the waves and storm " Be still."' In a letter to the Rev. D. M. M'Intyre, June 19th, 1891, he writes, 'I am not, and never was, a great or popular preacher. I have been only an earnest expounder of God's Word, longing to save sinners and edify the saved.' A friend remembers when a boy, hearing him preach in Regent Square, London, in the year 1850, and the deep impression made on his mind by the sermon—'The joys of the Man of Sorrows' (Acts ii. 26). A few weeks after he again heard him preach at Rait in Perthshire, and was struck with the fact that his sermon was not less able, and his delivery not less earnest in speaking to the quiet country audience than when addressing the 'great congregation' in Regent Square. If he spent a Sabbath in the country without preaching, he felt more tired at the close of the day than if he had preached three times. At Collace, Mrs. Bonar refers to his having preached nine times in one week ; and he himself writes in refusing an invitation to preach in Perth :—

'I see you thought you would bait your hook well to catch me by offering a triple service.'

'I go to Glasgow to Alexander Somerville on Monday, and to James Hamilton, London, immediately after, so you see I have some elements of the wandering Jew in my constitution. O that I were as wandering Paul and Barnabas ! They were Christ's true "knights - errant," *i.e.* servants (*knechte*), who went forth whithersoever He would.'

On one occasion he went to Blairgowrie to assist the Rev. Malcolm White at his Communion services. He arrived at six o'clock on Saturday evening, and hurriedly took some refreshment, so as to get to the top of Hatton Hill before dusk. From there he saw the beautiful view over the strath, but his chief object was to visit the birthplace of Donald Cargill, the martyr. Though it was late before he and Mr. White reached home, he showed little sign of weariness, and asked what his work was to be next day. When told, he said, ' I would not have left home had I known you had so little for me to do!' and a children's service had to be added to what most men would have considered quite sufficient work for one day.

In July 1890 he closes a letter to his son with these words: ' Why am I spared so long in health is a question I often ask. One thing I know—it must be that I may preach and commend Christ and Him crucified wherever and whenever it is in my power.'

In great loving-kindness God spared him the bitterness of being laid aside from his beloved work. Though feeble, voice and hand were still busy in the Master's service, when, at that Master's bidding, he left his work below for the ministry of the Upper Sanctuary, where still ' His servants serve Him.'